Off My
ROCKER

Off My
ROCKER

GRANDPARENTING AIN'T WHAT
IT USED TO BE

GRACIE MALONE

NAVPRESS

Bringing Truth to Life
P.O. Box 35001, Colorado Springs, Colorado 80935

OUR GUARANTEE TO YOU

We believe so strongly in the message of our books that we are making this quality guarantee to you. If for any reason you are disappointed with the content of this book, return the title page to us with your name and address and we will refund to you the list price of the book. To help us serve you better, please briefly describe why you were disappointed. Mail your refund request to: NavPress, P.O. Box 35002, Colorado Springs, CO 80935.

The Navigators is an international Christian organization. Our mission is to reach, disciple, and equip people to know Christ and to make Him known through successive generations. We envision multitudes of diverse people in the United States and every other nation who have a passionate love for Christ, live a lifestyle of sharing Christ's love, and multiply spiritual laborers among those without Christ.

NavPress is the publishing ministry of The Navigators. NavPress publications help believers learn biblical truth and apply what they learn to their lives and ministries. Our mission is to stimulate spiritual formation among our readers.

Cover design: David Carlson Design
Cover photo: Christopher Weil/Photonica
Creative Team: Nanci McAlister, Karen Lee-Thorp, Kathy Mosier, Pat Miller

Some of the anecdotal illustrations in this book are true to life and are included with the permission of the persons involved. All other illustrations are composites of real situations, and any resemblance to people living or dead is coincidental.

Unless otherwise identified, all Scripture quotations in this publication are taken from THE MESSAGE (MSG). Copyright © 1993, 1994, 1995, 1996, 2000, 2001, 2002. Used by permission of NavPress Publishing Group. Other versions used include the HOLY BIBLE: NEW INTERNATIONAL VERSION® (NIV®). Copyright © 1973, 1978, 1984 by International Bible Society. Used by permission of Zondervan Publishing House. All rights reserved; the New American Standard Bible (NASB), © The Lockman Foundation 1960, 1962, 1963, 1968, 1971, 1972, 1973, 1975, 1977; the Amplified New Testament (AMP), © The Lockman Foundation 1954, 1958; the New King James Version (NKJV). Copyright © 1982 by Thomas Nelson, Inc. Used by permission. All rights reserved; the Holy Bible, New Living Translation, (NLT) copyright © 1996. Used by permission of Tyndale House Publishers, Inc., Wheaton, Illinois 60189. All rights reserved; and the King James Version (KJV).

Malone, Gracie.
  Off my rocker : grandparenting ain't what it used to be / Gracie
Malone.-- 1st ed.
    p. cm.
Includes bibliographical references.
  ISBN 1-57683-389-5 (pbk.)
  1. Grandparents--Religious life. 2. Grandparenting--Religious
aspects--Christianity. I. Title.
  BV4528.5.M35 2003
  248.8'45--dc21

                                        2003004142

Printed in China

1 2 3 4 5 6 7 8 9 10 / 07 06 05 04 03

FOR A FREE CATALOG OF
NAVPRESS BOOKS & BIBLE STUDIES,
CALL 1-800-366-7788 (USA)
OR 1-416-499-4615 (CANADA)

To my mother
Velma Elizabeth Allen

Thank you for your patience . . .
>   for teaching me how to make biscuits from scratch,
>   to hem a skirt without the stitches showing,
>   to keep a good sense of humor even when everybody else
>   was losing theirs,
>   and for helping me understand that God is love and full
>   of grace.

Most of all, thank you for telling me again and again, "My
children are the greatest blessing of my life." Such
unconditional love keeps me centered. Your sweet
"Jesus smile" will bless me all the days of my life.

Contents

Grandmothers Then and Now

In the dim and distant past,
When life's tempo wasn't fast
Grandma used to rock and knit,
Crochet, tat and baby-sit.
When the kids were in a jam,
They could always count on Gram.
In an age of gracious living,
Grandma was the gal for giving.

Grandma now is at the gym,
Exercising to keep slim.
She's off touring with the "bunch,"
Taking clients out to lunch.
Driving North to ski or curl,
All her days are in a whirl.
Nothing seems to stop or block her,
Now that Grandma's off her rocker!

AUTHOR UNKNOWN[1]

Foreword

By Luke Malone (age 13)

WHEN MY grandmother told me she was going to write a book about grandparenting, I knew there would be lots of stories in it about me (because I'm the oldest grandchild and have been providing material the longest). I don't mind her writing about me as long as she doesn't write anything that would make me not wanna come out of my room for a couple of years! As my uncle Jason and I flipped through the pages of one of her last books, we realized our names were used quite a few times. So we teased my grandma about charging a nominal fee every time she used our names. If only we *had,* we could have been fairly rich by now.

I'm not the only one who could be making money off my grandma's stories. She also writes about my little brother, Connor, and my little sisters, Mary and Abby. Occasionally she writes about my cousins, Montana and Myles, and my stepsisters, Lexi and Ingrid. The stories are all true and are meant to help mothers and grandmothers look at the brighter side of parenting and grandparenting.

If anybody knows how to be a good grandmother, it's my Grandma Gracie. After raising three rowdy boys (including my dad), she now has six grandchildren and two stepgrandchildren. Somehow she has yet to lose her sanity and doesn't even have gray hair.

Since my grandmother is always telling stories about me, I think it's my turn to tell one about her. One year around Christmas, my dad's company had a party that included a trip to Six Flags Over Texas. When our family entered the park we decided to get into separate groups and do our own thing.

My dad and stepmom, Rachel, took Mary, Abby, and Ingrid to the merry-go-round, and Papa Joe took Connor and Lexi to ride the Runaway Mine Train. That left Grandma Gracie and me to formulate our own plan. Suddenly I had an idea: I challenged her to ride the G-Force. It's like an elevator with seats inside. It goes straight up about one hundred feet, then plummets to the ground fast enough to put your stomach in your mouth. Although a little nervous, Grandma Gracie accepted my challenge. We had to wait in line almost an hour, and the whole time I was telling her stories about how fast and scary the ride was. By the time it was our turn, she was already feeling sick to her stomach.

Once we got on the ride, they buckled us in and we started our climb toward the top. Grandma Gracie braced herself by pushing against the front of the elevator with her tennis shoes. Of course I was reassuring her the whole time by saying that the cars don't come off the track very often and as far as I knew, nobody had ever died on this ride.

Suddenly the car stopped and lurched forward. I saw a look of sheer terror cross my grandma's face. Then we dropped at a blinding speed, and before we knew it, we were on the ground. Although the ride was quick, it still rattled my grandma pretty badly. Shaking knees and all, she hobbled off the ride and headed for the ladies' room. I heard her mutter under her breath, "So that's what G-force means!"

That story is a taste of what this book is all about. I hope you enjoy reading my grandma's stories; I know they will help you get more out of the time you spend with your family.

In addition, maybe this book will help you become more like my grandma—someone who's bold and brave and maybe just a little bit crazy.

Special Thanks

THANK YOU to my precious grandchildren, Luke, Connor, Mary Catherine, Abby, Montana, and Myles, and to my two adorable stepgranddaughters, Alexis and Ingrid. You have brought so much joy into my life that I can't help sharing your stories with anyone who will listen.

Thanks to my three incredible sons, Matt, Mike, and Jason. You've been great sports. I'm glad you've all been able to keep your sense of humor, even when I'm telling on you.

To my husband, Joe: I owe a huge debt of gratitude for your patience and helpfulness. When Joe heard I was going to write this book, his first words were, "How can I help make it happen?" He shouldn't have asked! Before long, he was shopping for groceries, picking up dry cleaning, tidying up the kitchen, and even cooking an occasional breakfast. Thank you so much, Dear Hubby.

My deep appreciation to Dr. John Morris, our friend-counselor-pastor extraordinaire. Thanks for words of encouragement when I felt out of my comfort zone, for sharing deep scriptural insights, and for your prayers. You have taught me the meaning of *koinonia*.

Thank you to my agent, Lee Hough, and to the great team at Alive Communications. Thanks for believing in me and doing an "un-stinkin-believable" job of representing me.

Thanks to Terry Behimer, Karen Lee-Thorp, and the team at

NavPress for helping me produce a better product than I could even dream possible.

Lastly, a special thanks to my girlfriends, Becky Freeman, Ellie Kay, Fran Sandin, Julie Barnhill, Brenda Waggoner, Pat Routen, and Rachel St. John-Gilbert. You each came to my rescue in different ways at different times. Without your support I would literally be "Off My Rocker."

Introduction

WHEN MY friend Vern invited me to join her for lunch, I thought it was just that—lunch. But when I arrived at the restaurant and several other friends showed up, I realized this was going to be a party. Conversation was buzzing as we gathered in the lobby. I fell in line behind Vern as the waiter led us to a table decorated with spring flowers and balloons. By the time we'd picked our spots and settled in our chairs, I was in full party mode. I had no idea what we were celebrating, but I sure was having fun. It wasn't until I noticed the lettering on the silver balloon that I realized the party was for me. Apparently, we were celebrating my recently acquired contract for *Off My Rocker!*

As the balloon's message, "Congratulations, You Did It," bobbed up and down in the center of the table, I swallowed hard. I thought about how dear these friends had become. Then I realized how appropriate this gathering was. This group of friends was a microcosm of my target audience—women of all ages with one thing in common: a fierce love for their children and grandchildren.

While the waiter took our orders, my eyes scanned the faces of the women in the circle. Vern, a great-grandmother (she prefers "g-grandmother" for some reason) barely in her sixties, was decked out in an orange and purple silk blouse and size five jeans. Her jewelry flashed as she handed me a card. Seated next to Vern was her daughter Terri, looking as if she had just stepped out of a fashion magazine with her capris and sun-bronzed skin. Nobody would have guessed she was a forty-something-year-old grandmother of two. Next to Terri was her daughter-in-law Kara, vivacious mother of eighteen-month-old Grace, who occupied the high chair at the end of the table. Terri's daughter Leslie, an "all-American girl," was opening a package of crackers to console her twenty-month-old son, Corbin. (We're not opposed to having at least one male friend accompany us at our parties!) Next to me sat Sue Ann, a snazzy, upscale interior decorator and, most importantly, mother of three daughters. She couldn't wait to tell us about the basketball tournament her daughter Chelsea had played in the night before. Her team had won—a victory made even more precious because the team plays from their wheelchairs.

In case you've lost count, that circle of eight friends included two grandmothers, one g-grandmother, a mother of teens, two mothers of toddlers, and the two toddlers themselves. I couldn't hold back a giggle as I realized there was enough energy around that table to ignite a stick of dynamite—or at least make a major difference in the world our little ones inhabit. And so it is with grandmothers today. They are younger than ever—according to AARP, the average grandmother is a mere forty-seven—and they are doing more with and for their grandchildren than ever before.

Grandmothers of today are a new breed. You'll find them gliding along on roller blades, working out at the gym, running behind a Baby Jogger, and managing Fortune 500 companies. The only time you'll find them in a rocking chair is when they're reading to their grandchild or lacing up their tennis shoes.

It is to these women and countless other kindred spirits that I have written *Off My Rocker*. If you are a mother who wants her child to feel that one-of-a-kind bond with her grandmother, or if you are a grandmother or g-grandmother seeking a better relationship with your grandchild, this book is for you. Its stories will encourage you, help you, and make you laugh.

Within each chapter, there's a section called "On Grandma's Lap" that offers ideas for meaningful interaction with your little ones. (Grandma's lap is the perfect place for a child to connect with the grandmother, a place where security and trust are developed.) Another section, "Grandma's Tips," is designed for those grandparents who are more involved in the parenting of their progeny. (Did you know that over four million grandmothers in the United States are primary caregivers for their children's children? And, of course, many more provide day care or weekend support.) This section suggests books, games, conversation starters, websites, and other ideas to make grandmothering easier. Finally, and most importantly, I've included "Timeless Truth"—a section with insight and words of encouragement from the Bible.

Grandparenting is not what it used to be—it's better. It's hands-on, up close and personal, fast paced, vitamin fortified, and fun! May you find in *Off My Rocker* the help, hope, and humor you need along the way.

My Children's Children

When your newborn grandchild holds your little finger
in his little fist, you're hooked for life.

—ANDY ROONEY

ONE MORNING the phone rang persistently as I dried my hands on a kitchen towel and located the receiver buried beneath a pile of magazines. It was our oldest son, Matt. "If you hurry," he blurted out excitedly, "you can make it for the birth of your grandson." I jumped in the car and headed for the hospital—a drive that would take almost an hour.

As I sped down the highway from our rural home near Greenville toward North Dallas, my mind drifted back to the time when my first child was born. When sharp labor pains woke me in the middle of the night, the thrill of becoming a mommy—a dream I'd cherished since I was old enough to cradle a baby doll in my arms—was suddenly overshadowed by the reality of giving birth. I was scared silly as I grabbed my overnight bag and set out for the hospital. However, as soon as I settled in a bed in the maternity ward, the labor slowed down and I spent the next twenty-four hours trying to get the process started again.

While I waited, Joe, my nervous young hubby, paced the floor and tried to concentrate on the out-of-date magazines in the lobby. Instead, he found himself hugging the porcelain throne in the men's room as his nervousness hit his stomach! Even after my labor resumed, I think Joe suffered more than I did. Every time I felt a pain, the doctor gave me a whiff of gas and I dozed into a peaceful sleep. Joe, on the other hand, suffered vicariously with nothing to anesthetize his pain. Eventually, at the doctor's suggestion, he went outside and took a nap in the backseat of our '57 Chevy. He came back just as the attendants whisked me off to the delivery room. The next morning I woke up from a drug-induced state and discovered I'd given birth to a six-pound, eleven-ounce boy. We named him Matt.

Joe assured me little Matt was just fine. He'd seen him— through the thick glass of the nursery window. Not until five days later, after we brought the baby home, did he get to hold his son.

Mothers of the little ones born in that hospital were granted *a few* more privileges than the dads were. Still, every decision rested in the hands of the hospital staff. When the nurse determined I was alert enough to hold my newborn—more than twenty hours after the baby's birth—Joe was ushered out of the room and little Matt was brought in and placed in my eager arms. He was tightly swaddled in a blue blanket. Even his arms were pinned down in a fold of flannel. I have to admit, seeing my baby looking like a pint-sized mummy brought out the rebel in me. I removed the diaper pin holding the bundle together and allowed him to wiggle and stretch freely. But as soon as feeding time was over, I quickly repackaged my baby and handed him over submissively to the nurse.

After five days, the doctor declared me well and competent—at least enough to take our baby home.

Two years after Matt was born, we had another son, Mike, and a few years later yet another, Jason. I had become the mother of three little boys, none of whom caused me much discomfort at birth. They were literally born while I was sleeping. Even though I had given birth three times, I could still say with Prissy of *Gone With the Wind*, "I don't know nothin' about birthin' babies."

❈❈❈❈❈❈

My, how things have changed in the maternity ward in just one generation! Today moms know *everything* about "birthin' babies," and daddies do, too. The emphasis is no longer upon pain-free delivery but on "natural childbirth." I remember my mother talking about home deliveries done the natural way, so this *new* concept seemed like a step back in time to me. To be honest, the idea of allowing nature to take its course wasn't all that appealing to me—until I witnessed the natural process up close and personal.

When I arrived at the hospital, I whipped into a parking place, pushed through the double front doors, and headed down the hall marked "Maternity." Rounding the corner into the waiting room, I spotted Matt decked out in hospital scrubs with a surgical mask hanging loosely around his neck. Apparently, childbirth classes had prepared him to be a fully participating member of the delivery team. "Follow me," he whispered as he opened the door and escorted me into the birthing room.

My daughter-in-law was nestled in a contraption that looked more like Joe's recliner than a hospital bed. She was tired from the hard work of labor but fully awake and smiling as she extended a tiny bundle in my direction. "Want to hold him?" she asked.

Yes! Of course I did.

Gently taking the baby from his mother's arms, I felt my heart warming up to this hands-on style of "birthin' babies." Baby Luke was warm, wiggling, and obviously only minutes old. I'd forgotten how small a newborn baby is, barely big enough to fit in the crook of a woman's arm. As I pulled him close, I was suddenly overcome with love, joy, hope, and a swelling sense of pride—the same feelings I'd experienced when I held my own newborn sons. I choked back the lump rising in my throat.

I examined the tiny features of my newborn grandson: slate-blue eyes straining to focus in the soft light, a perfect heart-shaped mouth, and a tiny upturned nose. I folded back the corner of the blue flannel blanket to get a look at his ears. The moment I saw them I felt joy rising in my soul like bubbles in a glass of champagne. My grandson was sporting a matched set of the *family ears*—carbon copies of his daddy's ears, miniature versions of my own.

Ours are rather handsome ears, if I do say so myself—a bit on the small side with a tiny crimp on top. As my finger traced the rim of those splendid ears, the family "earmark," so to speak, I marveled at the wonder of God's creation.

The words of the psalmist came to mind: "You made all the delicate, inner parts of my body and knit me together in my mother's womb. Thank you for making me so wonderfully complex! Your workmanship is marvelous—and how well I know it" (Psalm

139:13-14, NLT). Some biblical scholars describe the developing baby as "intricately and curiously wrought [as if embroidered with various colors]" (Psalm 139:15, AMP). The thought that God, the awesome Creator of the universe, had been intricately involved in the design of my precious grandson—from the tip of his toe to the crimp of his ear—brought tears of joy to my eyes.

I lifted the tiny bundle close to my lips and whispered against the soft folds of skin, "Luke, I'm your grandmother. I love you. I always will, no matter what."

In response, he stretched and yawned, then turned his face toward my bosom as if to ask, *Got milk?* Since my answer was an unspoken but obvious *no,* he immediately took matters into his own hands—literally. He brought one tiny hand to his face, slipped his thumb into his mouth, and started sucking. He lifted his other hand upward and touched the side of his head, right above his left ear, as if to say, *Nice ears, huh, Grandma?*

I couldn't hold back an outburst of joy as I realized this wasn't the first time I'd seen Luke make that gesture—not on this unforgettable day, but in a video of a sonogram Matt had brought to our house months earlier.

I remember how we all gathered around the television screen and observed in rapt silence little Luke's movements, his tiny body only six inches long. He twisted and turned in the embryonic fluid as if he were swimming in a warm bath. After a few moments we were not only convinced he was a boy, but we were also captivated by his charm. His hand moved close to the camera and we counted five little fingers. One hand went to his mouth. Then his tiny thumb, smaller than a pea, brushed across his lips and slipped into his mouth. His other arm stretched upward, his hand touching the side of his head.

As I saw him make this same movement on the day of his birth, my heart overflowed with the purest form of love I'd ever experienced. The tiny baby we had adored while he was still in his mother's womb had made a grand entrance into my world and stolen my heart.

With the birth of this little boy, our family had come full circle, making our own revolution in the great circle of life. A new generation was born that day—one that would bear our name, and, besides that, one that would proudly display our ears!

The family dynamics changed dramatically with the new addition. Without even applying for the job, everybody assumed new roles, complete with new titles. My son was now Luke's Daddy. My hubby had become Grandpa. Our other two sons were Uncles. And I had become a *Grandmother*. With the title came an overwhelming sense of responsibility. I wanted to be the *World's Best Grandmother*. Yet I actually knew very little about grandparenting; I'd never read a book or taken a course on the subject. In the years to come I would learn more about my role, little by little—mostly by trial and error and lots of prayer.

Since Luke's birth, I've been in the waiting room during the arrival of five additional grandchildren. Luke became big brother to Connor. They welcomed two little sisters, Mary Catherine and Abby. Our son Mike and daughter-in-law Jeanna presented us with two little boys—Montana and Myles.

Each child came into the world with his or her own unique characteristics and temperament. Each came with a unique story that I hope to tell one of these days.

Speaking of storytelling, nobody tells the story of her birth better than our youngest granddaughter, Abby.

Shortly after her fifth birthday, I pulled her onto my lap, kissed her on her forehead, and said, "Abby, I remember when you were born. I was there. You were the cutest little thing. . . . "

At this point, she interrupted boisterously by exclaiming, "I know, I know! I was in my mom's tummy trying to get out and my mom was puuushhhing and puuushhhing." Abby let out a huge grunt, *"Aaaaarrrrrrgghhhhh!"* With wild hand gestures and an animated tone, she continued. "Then I gave her two big karate chops—*Yahhh, Yahhh*—and out I came." She brushed out a wrinkle in her skirt, grinned, and added, "Ta-dah!"

Ta-dah, indeed!

Seems this grandma *still* has a lot to learn about "birthin' babies"!

※※※※※※

I'm grateful I live near my adult children and have been present each time a grandchild was born. Unfortunately, some grandmothers do not have that privilege. Maybe you live a long distance from your children and heard the greatly anticipated announcement over the phone. You may have children who adopted your precious grandchild, and the birth announcement came a few days after the baby's arrival.

I also realize that some babies are born in circumstances that are less than ideal. Thousands of single moms give birth every day without a loving coach to stand beside them and encourage them. And some babies are born with medical problems that cause confusion and pain not only for the parents but for the grandparents as well.

But regardless of the circumstances, there is much to celebrate with the birth of any child. Every single one of them is designed, like an intricate piece of colorful embroidery, by the loving hands of the Master Designer of the universe.

Your precious grandchild is God's priceless work of art—and someone to be cherished.

> Great is the LORD, and highly to be praised, and His
> greatness is unsearchable. One generation shall
> praise Your works to another, and shall declare Your
> mighty acts. (Psalm 145:3-4, NASB)

ON GRANDMA'S LAP

▶ "On grandma's lap" is one place in the world where every grandchild should feel totally accepted and perfectly beautiful. In today's society, too much emphasis is placed upon physical perfection. Even very young children begin to worry about their size and physical features. Grandmothers can be a stabilizing force in this area. Compliment your grandchildren. Talk about God's creativity and the uniqueness of each of His children.

▶ Collect memorabilia concerning the birth of each grandchild. You can compile these in a scrapbook or keepsake box. Include the birth announcement, newspaper clippings, and the church bulletin. Newspaper or magazine articles that show the culture or current events at the time of your grandbaby's birth will be interesting to the child later on. When your grandchild becomes old enough to appreciate it, share the contents of your keepsake box with him or her.

▶ Compile a journal of your thoughts about the day of his or her birth. Or, write a letter to the child, telling about your feelings and thoughts. When the child is older, read your journal or letter or present it on the child's sixteenth birthday.

▶ Talk with your grandchildren about the day they were born. Tell them how you felt, what made an impression on you, how they responded to your touch. Talk about how other family members reacted to their birth.

Grandma's Tips

Ten Ways Grandmothers Can Make Birthdays Easier

1. Offer to stay in the waiting room with the siblings during the birth. Pack a bag with healthy snacks and a few carefully selected toys for the kids to play with while they wait. Include books, coloring books, card games, and even a Nerf ball or Nerf frisbee to work off pent-up energy.

2. If the parents prefer, be willing to keep the older children at home. Plan some games or special treats to make the day memorable.

3. If you live out of town, send the siblings a care package with the same kinds of toys and nonperishable snacks.

4. Offer to help after the new baby comes home from the hospital. Let your children make the call about how long your visit needs to be. For some new parents a two-week visit might be right; others can't wait to tackle the parenting role on their own.

5. Be careful about giving unsolicited advice. Remember the new mom is a walking kettle of hormones and is also tired and emotional. The best grandmas will give the new mom plenty of support and emotional space, not reading too much into her moodiness or her need to be alone or to nap.

6. Prepare a few nutritious, not-too-fattening meals for the new mom (and other family members). She will probably be ready for some food that will nourish but also help her begin to shrink her waistline.

7. Stock the freezer with easy-to-prepare foods from the grocery store.

8. Offer to run some errands, such as picking up the cleaning or a few items from the store.

9. If you purchase a gift for the new baby, bring along a small gift or book for the other children as well.

10. Take the older siblings shopping so they can buy a gift for the new baby.

TIMELESS TRUTH

When our grandchildren arrive, all the maternal instincts we possess rise up in our souls once again. We not only want to be with our grandkids to enjoy them, but we also feel an overwhelming need to protect them and see that they get the very best in life. As we deal with these complicated emotions, there is no greater comfort than knowing God is watching over and caring for our little ones. He loves them more than we do! And He is intimately involved in every aspect of their lives.

Psalm 139 tells us in vivid detail just how much He sees and knows them:

> O LORD, you have searched me
>   and you know me.
> You know when I sit and when I rise;
>   you perceive my thoughts from afar.
> You discern my going out and my lying down;
>   you are familiar with all my ways.
> Before a word is on my tongue
>   you know it completely, O LORD.
> You hem me in—behind and before;
>   you have laid your hand upon me.
> Such knowledge is too wonderful for me,
>   too lofty for me to attain.
> Where can I go from your Spirit?
>   Where can I flee from your presence?
> If I go up to the heavens, you are there;
>   if I make my bed in the depths, you are there.
> If I rise on the wings of the dawn,
>   if I settle on the far side of the sea,
> even there your hand will guide me,
>   your right hand will hold me fast.
> If I say, "Surely the darkness will hide me
>   and the light become night around me,"
> even the darkness will not be dark to you;
>   the night will shine like the day,
>   for darkness is as light to you. (1-12, NIV)

- He sees when they sit down or when they stand up.
- He knows their inward thoughts—the motions of their minds as well as their bodies.
- He is beside them in their running and resting.
- He is with them when they are awake or asleep.

- He sees everything they do, whether it is done openly or secretly.
- He knows their words—spoken and unspoken.
- He goes before them and behind them.
- He holds them in His hand wherever they are—on a mountain-top or in some deep valley, soaring above the earth in an airplane or traversing the bottom of the ocean floor in a submarine.
- He sees them in the darkness and in the brightest sunlight.

> For you created my inmost being;
>   you knit me together in my mother's womb.
> I praise you because I am fearfully and wonder-
>   fully made;
>   your works are wonderful,
>   I know that full well.
> My frame was not hidden from you
>   when I was made in the secret place.
> When I was woven together in the depths of the earth,
>   your eyes saw my unformed body.
> All the days ordained for me
>   were written in your book
>   before one of them came to be. (13-16, NIV)

- He created their innermost longings and passions as well as their outward features.
- He formed their shape and substance—their "frame" (tall or short, strong or frail) as well as their mental faculties and personality traits.
- He directs the pilgrimage of their lives—from before they were born until the end of their days.

> How precious to me are your thoughts, O God!
>   How vast is the sum of them!

> Were I to count them,
> > they would outnumber the grains of sand.
> When I awake,
> > I am still with you. (17-18, NIV)

- God thinks about our grandchildren continually—thoughts without number, beginning in eternity past and continuing until the end of time.
- He is always with them. His love is infinite.

What's in a Name?

The sole purpose of a middle name
is so children can tell when they're really in trouble.
—DENNIS FAKES

WHEN LESLIE named her first baby the family surname, Pierce, her parents, Linda and Carl, were beside themselves with joy. Linda couldn't wait to share the news with me during a recent visit. "Gracie," she began, "it seems so natural to call our new grandbaby by our last name. It brings back memories of when our sons, David and Bryan, were growing up and their coaches and friends called them 'Pierce.'"

I remembered. My own sons were often referred to as "Malone."

"Besides that," Linda continued, "it means the family name is passed down to another generation—not only by our sons, but on our daughter's branch of the family tree as well."

I understood perfectly. Family names are important to folks like Linda and me. They make us feel connected to our roots. We think it's important for family newcomers to know we have ancestors that go way back in time. Family ties also remind us of God's faithfulness and His sustaining grace through the years. What could make a grandmother more proud than having her grandchildren bear the family name?

After Linda and I said good-bye and I headed toward home, I thought about how my hubby and I had decided to give our second son the name Allen, my maiden name. We used Allen as a middle name in combination with Michael. The tradition was passed down to one of our grandsons, Connor Allen. Having a family name as a child's second name is a more subtle way to remember our fore-fathers. It's a shame, though, that a child's middle name is so seldom spoken. Unless the child gets in big trouble, most people won't have a clue what name occupies the central position. The family name is not concealed with Linda and Carl's grandbaby, however. Pierce is right out there, up front, and useable—just the way his grandparents like it.

By the way, Pierce is a little boy.

I know what you might be thinking: With a name like that, he'd have to be a boy! But in case you haven't noticed, it's trendy these days to give one's child a moniker commonly thought of as a last name, and surprisingly, not all of them are boys. I know little boys named Jackson, Tyler, Harrison, and Hunter and girls named Taylor, Cameron, Madison, and McKenzie. I've also heard that some grandmothers are not pleased when their little girls are labeled with such sturdy appellations. It would help those discon-tented grandmas to think back to some of the fads of former days.

It could be that today's picks are a reaction to the fluffy names of the sixties. In those days, girls' names often ended with an i—Terri,

Patti, or Wendi, for example. Common names for little boys ended with y. My sister Lois explained, "I want my little boys to have names that sound playful and fun!" She paused before adding, "But I'm giving them professional-sounding middle names in case one of them wants to be a doctor, or a lawyer, or the president of the United States." Hence her three sons are Jerry Glenn, Tommy Anthony, and Larry Edward.

Today's names-with-substance include some with a scope as big as the great outdoors—names destined to put them on the map. I've met kids named Dakota, Austin, Dallas, Cheyenne, Sierra, and Albuquerque. (Okay, I'm kidding about Albuquerque!) But there are some pretty big names out there—names that are a mouthful for grandmothers.

I'll never forget the day our son Mike introduced his firstborn son to us. A lump rose in my throat when I saw our six-foot-two son strolling toward us with a tiny bundle tucked under his arm like a football. Then he stooped, opened the blanket, and tenderly spoke the baby's name: "We're going to call him Montana—Montana Ryan." I blinked as I imagined calling this tiny baby something as rugged and unbridled as "Montana."

It was a name Mike had come up with when he was in high school and admired the great athletes Joe Montana and Nolan Ryan. Now, years later, our daughter-in-law Jeanna was in complete agreement. This child would not be called "Monty" or "Mo" or any other shortened version. He was Montana. At first, I had a hard time calling this little tyke such a majestic name. But as I followed the wishes of his parents, I found myself actually liking the name. Now that he's seven, it's clear he was aptly named. The child is a great little athlete who loves the outdoors and wide-open spaces.

Names became important to me when I was in high school, too, especially when I began dating my first serious boyfriend—the guy who would eventually become my husband. Even when I was still in the fantasy phase of our relationship, I would write my first name with his last on my book covers and on pieces of scrap paper—Gracie Malone, Mrs. Joe Malone. I liked the sound of it and I loved the way it looked when I wrote it in my best swirly handwriting.

Once I married and changed my name to his, I started coming up with names for our future children—first names that went well with Malone. All my choices began with the letter M. In those days, names had become a sort of fashion statement; the first name needed to coordinate with the last. So, on my scratch pad, I wrote in my very best handwriting a plethora of "M" names to eventually choose from: Matthew, Mark, Mike, Molly, Mindy, Megan. Unfortunately, I never got to use a single girl's name. But I stuck with my choices for boys and ended up calling our firstborn, Matt and our second, Mike. By the time our third son came along, twelve years after our second, I'd tired of yada yada and went a completely different direction, naming him Jason.

Some people stuck with the matching name phenomenon much longer. When we lived in Paris, Texas, we were fascinated to learn that our pastor, Dr. James Semple, and his wife, Betty, had given all their children names beginning with the letter J. Even today, thirty-something years later, I still remember the names of those children—Jimmy, Jon, Jan, Jill, Jenene, and JoNel. Such is the beauty of using alliteration. The names are easy to remember—at least for me. But sometimes I couldn't help wondering how many times that eloquent preacher stuttered when he called the kids for dinner. We moved away from Paris before our preacher friend had grandchildren, but we heard the tradition lasted well into the next generation with a whole passel of children, including Jennifer, Joseph, Jeffrey, Julie, Jay, Jared, Janae, John Mark, Jerica, Jessica, Jonathan, Jamie Kate, Jami Anne, Jeremy, Jill Beth, Joshua Jacob, Joel, Jordan, James, and . . . and Leah. I guess it was inevitable that the family memory bank would eventually be on "J" overload. However, during a recent conversation, Dr. Semple told me they are expecting two great-grandchildren. "Who knows where the tradition may go from here," he commented in a lighthearted tone.

Even though as a young mother my first criteria for name choosing was its beginning letter, I also wanted my choices to have spiritual significance. We knew that Matthew means "Gift of God." I thought it was just perfect to call our precious child such a divine thing. (I thought about changing his name to something more of-this-earth only once or twice as he was growing up.) Before we dubbed our second son Michael, we found out it means "Sent from God." Jason means "Healer." Before he was even born, I envisioned this small child coming into a troubled world and making a major difference, bringing healing.

When I selected the name Matthew (more than forty years ago, mind you), I'd only heard the name used once. There's probably a gazillion kids named Matt in the world today, but I want you to know, *I'm the one who started that trend.* I thought Mike and Jason were unique, too. However, a few years after our children's names were duly recorded, filed, and well used, I read an article in the newspaper claiming, "The three most frequently used names today are Matt, Mike, and Jason." I shrugged my shoulders and thought, *So much for originality.*

By the time our boys reached the teen years, the idea of giving kids names with spiritual significance had morphed into something more "totally biblical." Everybody needed a name straight out of the Good Book. Parents weren't settling for simple New Testament names either. Mark, Timothy, and Paul didn't have the spiritual clout parents were looking for. They began reaching back into Old Testament lineages, picking heavy-duty names like Isaiah, Elijah, and Jeremiah. A few parents chose the patriarchs — Moses, Abraham, Isaac, or Jacob.

Even though we older folk had to appreciate names with eternal significance, to be honest, some of us felt it was a bit much. My friend Becky says her mother, Ruthie, gave an audible gasp when she announced the name of her second little boy.

"His name is Ezekiel," Becky declared. "We're going to call him Zeke."

"Becky!" Ruthie chided. "That sounds like a tall, skinny farmer in overalls."

Ruthie was right on at least two counts. Zeke turned out to be tall and skinny. But he's a builder instead of a farmer.

※※※※※※

What is it about names anyway? Where is God while trends come and go? Does He know what's going on? Does He care?

I did a little research and discovered that God is more than aware of our naming scenarios. He is not only watching from His exalted position behind the scenes, but He's overseeing the whole process—nudging a certain direction, influencing the selection. So when struggling parents finally settle on *the perfect* name, it is the Heavenly Father's choice as well. I also found out that names have been used since the beginning of time. In the Garden of Eden, God called the first man Adam. He in turn gave his new partner a name with special meaning, Eve—"the mother of all the living" (Genesis 3:20). Throughout Bible times, names with significance and deep spiritual meaning were assigned to individuals. Sometimes, after some lofty spiritual experience or in preparation for an important task, God changed a person's name from a down-to-earth title to something with a heavenly dimension.

But the most significant name change will happen at the end of time—that point in history when God gathers His people in the Celestial City and pays tribute to faithful believers. In an awards ceremony that will far outshine the giving of the Olympic gold, God Himself will present each victor a smooth, white stone engraved with his or her name.[1] The trophy itself will not be valuable—it won't be gold, silver, or bronze, but simply a piece of stone. Rather, it will be the *name* inscribed upon it that will give it value. That is the trophy! It will be a *new* name, a name so personal and intimate that only God and the one receiving it will know what it is.

Sometimes I wonder what my new name will be. Will it be simple or eloquent? Will it rhyme with other members of the family of God? Will all our names begin with the same Hebrew letter? Probably not! But it will be a family name. And when I hear my secret name uttered by lips that spoke the world into existence, I can only imagine how I might feel. My face will turn toward Him, our eyes will connect, and in that moment, I will know with certainty that I am His unique and cherished child. *I will know it because of my name.*

Meanwhile, as we live out our lives here on planet Earth, parents will struggle with what to call their progeny. Grandparents may wince at first as we move past our preconceived notions, but eventually we'll learn to appreciate our children's choices. Most kids will like the name given them; others will grow into it. But, alas, some will just have to wait till eternity to settle the matter.

Take, for example, my great-nephew.

One Sunday afternoon after church, my brother Charles and his five-year-old grandson, Colt, were waiting in the parking lot for the other family members to come. As they leaned against the car's door, the boy struck up a conversation: "You know what, Granddad? I don't like my name."

"Is that right?" Charles answered. "Why not?"

"Oh, I don't know. I just wish Mom and Dad had named me something else." Colt shifted from one foot to the other. "You know, more like other kids."

Charles pressed the issue: "Well, Colt, if you could change your name, what would you choose?"

Colt shrugged his shoulders and continued, "I just wish my name was Matthew, or Mark, or Luke, or . . . or . . . Acts!"

> I have redeemed you; I have called you by name;
> you are Mine! (Isaiah 43:1, NASB)

ON GRANDMA'S LAP

▶ Pull your grandchild onto your lap and talk about his or her name. Tell how the name was selected. Did his or her parents have a difficult time deciding? Is he or she named after a relative?

▶ Locate a book that contains a list of names and their meanings. Some of these books give a spiritual meaning as well as the background of the name. Talk with your grandchildren about what their names mean. Some information about the background of family names can be found in an encyclopedia.

▶ Some bookstores sell plaques displaying a person's name, the meaning of the name, and a related verse of Scripture. Consider buying your grandchildren one of these plaques, or make a plaque yourself. Seeing their name proudly displayed on the walls of their home—or yours—will brighten their days.

▶ It's fun and completely okay to call your grandchildren by nicknames or "pet" names. Even though they may act like they don't like your made-up names for them, they'll feel loved and special. Pull one of your grandkids onto your lap, give her a big hug, and call her "sweet feet" or something equally as silly. You'll likely be rewarded with a sheepish smile or a giggle.

Grandma's Tips

NAME GAMES

▶ Have your grandchildren read some of the names from the first few chapters of 1 Chronicles or from the first chapter of Matthew. Try to pronounce some of the funny-sounding names such as Mibsam, Husham, Heman, Gazez, Jehoshaphat, and Zerubbabel. Try to imagine what each person did. Was Heman a weight lifter? Maybe Husham was a babysitter!

▶ Try using some of the names to make up knock-knock jokes (Knock, knock. Who's there? Euodia. Euodia who? Euodia of Yo Feet!). Or play the name game (Mibsam, Mibsam-bo-bibsam, banana-fana-fo-fibsam, etc.). Sounding out the names and talking about them is fun, but it also lets your little ones know that these ancient names belong to real people who loved God.

▶ Encourage your older grandchildren to search the Web to learn more about their extended family. Try the following genealogy sites for kids:

www.geocities.com/EnchantedForest/5283/genekids.htm

www.home.earthlink.net/~howardorjeff/instruct.htm

Timeless Truth

One reason I know names are important is because God has so many of them. They're more than just titles; they are God's description of Himself. Throughout history, whenever His people needed some special revelation of His power or presence, God would disclose one of His names. People felt comforted and empowered when God revealed His name, for it told them something about Who He was and how He would take care of them. The names of God are important to believers today as well. They remind us that God is active in all the affairs of our lives.

It's not easy to find these names in modern translations of the Bible, and they often sound funny because of their Hebrew flavor. Nevertheless, it's a fascinating study. The Father wants us to know Him—by name—so we will instinctively run to Him with all our needs. The psalmist declares, "Those who know your name will trust in you" (Psalm 9:10, NIV).

- His name is *Elohim*—A plural term that indicates God's three-in-one nature: Father, Son, and Holy Spirit. *Elohim* reveals God's power and might. In your Bible it will be written "God."

  > First this: God [Elohim] created the Heavens and Earth. *(Genesis 1:1)*

  > Attention, Israel! GOD [YHWH], our God [Elohim]! GOD [YHWH] the one and only! (Deuteronomy 6:4)

- His name is *El Elyon*—His first name *El* is a singular term for God and means Supreme Majesty. *Elyon* reveals Him as the Sovereign Ruler of the universe. Knowing that God is in control is a great source of comfort to His people.

  > I, Nebuchadnezzar . . . blessed the High God [El Elyon], thanking and glorifying God, who lives forever.

  > His sovereign rule lasts and lasts,
  >   his kingdom never declines and falls. (Daniel 4:34)

- His name is *El Shaddai*—God of grace, mercy, and infinite resources. *El Shaddai* nourishes and satisfies us. When you see the name "Almighty" in your Bible, it is our *El Shaddai*.

> When Abram was ninety-nine years old, the LORD
> appeared to him and said, "I am God Almighty [El
> Shaddai]; walk before me and be blameless."
> (Genesis 17:1, NIV)

> Because of your father's God, who helps you,
> because of the Almighty [El Shaddai], who blesses
> you with blessings of the heavens above, blessings
> of the deep that lies below, blessings of the breast
> and womb. (Genesis 49:25, NIV)

• His name is *El Roi*—This name reveals God as the One who sees everything. Even though this name is only recorded once, it reveals something important. God sees you and me at all times, observing everything that happens in our lives. (That could be a bit disconcerting at times, but it is comforting when you're lonely or feel nobody cares.)

> She answered GOD by name, praying to the God who
> spoke to her, "You're the God [El] who sees [Roi] me!"

> "Yes! He saw me; and then I saw him!" (Genesis 16:13)

• He is *Adonai*—Lord. *Adonai* is a title that reveals God as the Master. Jesus is our "King of kings and Lord of lords." Usually *Adonai* is written with a capital *L* and lowercase *ord*.

> This word of GOD came to Abram in a vision: "Don't be
> afraid, Abram. I'm your shield. Your reward will be
> grand!" Abram said, "GOD, Master [Adonai], what use
> are your gifts as long as I'm childless?" (Genesis 15:1-2)

> The word of GOD to my Lord [Adonai]: "Sit alongside
> me here on my throne until I make your enemies a
> stool for your feet." (Psalm 110:1)

- His name is *Jehovah*—"I AM." *Jehovah* reveals God as the self-existent, ever-present One—the total essence of everything. The great I AM is the atmosphere in which we live and breathe. Pious Jews spelled *Jehovah* "YHWH," a name so reverent they were prohibited from even saying it. In the New Testament, Jesus claimed to be God when He said, "Before Abraham was born, I am!" (John 8:58, NIV). *Jehovah* is usually translated LORD (small caps).

> God said to Moses, "I AM WHO I AM. This is what you
> are to say to the Israelites: 'I AM has sent me to you.'"
> God also said to Moses, "Say to the Israelites, 'The
> LORD [Jehovah], the God of your fathers—the God of
> Abraham, the God of Isaac and the God of Jacob—
> has sent me to you.' This is my name forever, the
> name by which I am to be remembered from genera-
> tion to generation." (Exodus 3:14-15, NIV)

- His name is *Jehovah-Jireh*—"The LORD Will Provide." This name of God reminds us that He is always present and gives the strength or supply for whatever He asks us to do. *Jehovah-Jireh* is our covenant-keeping God.

> Abraham looked up and there in a thicket he saw a
> ram caught by its horns. He went over and took the
> ram and sacrificed it as a burnt offering instead of his
> son. So Abraham called that place The LORD

> [Jehovah] Will Provide [Jireh]. And to this day it is
> said, "On the mountain of the LORD [Jehovah] it will
> be provided." (Genesis 22:13-14, NIV)

- His name is *Jehovah-Rapha*—*Jehovah-Rapha* is the great remedy
  for those in need of physical, moral, or spiritual healing. *Jehovah*
  means ever-present. *Rapha* means healer. God is the healer of
  mankind. Jesus is the Great Physician.

> GOD said, "If you listen, listen obediently to how GOD
> tells you to live in his presence, obeying his com-
> mandments and keeping all his laws, then I won't
> strike you will all the diseases that I inflicted on the
> Egyptians; I am GOD [Jehovah] your healer [Rapha]."
> (Exodus 15:26)

God has many other names. If you'd like to know more, consult
one of the following books: *Lord, I Want to Know You* by Kay Arthur
or *The Names of God* by Nathan Stone.

There is no better way to know God than to know Him "by
name" just as He knows us. Next time you bow your head to pray,
address God by one of His personal names—the name that means
the most to you.

From the Mouths of Babes

My mind not only wanders, sometimes it leaves completely.
—BARBARA JOHNSON

AFTER A long shopping excursion with his mom, our grandson Luke, six, spoke for tired moms everywhere when he sank into the car's backseat and proclaimed, "I think God should've made everything cost one dollar, and everything fat free and no traffic!"

It wasn't the first time, nor would it be the last, when one of our pint-sized kids spouted liberal doses of grown-up wisdom to the aging members of the Malone clan. While we're fussing and fuming over a perplexing situation, they are coming up with some sage solution. Such pronouncements confirm the truth that wisdom does indeed come from the "mouths of babes." Most grandparents can identify. We're continually amazed by the witty and wise contributions our grandkids make to our otherwise routine ramblings.

When I think about my grandchildren growing up and becoming wise, I can't help but think about the childhood of Jesus. He matured the same way our own kids do—"in wisdom and stature, and in favor with God and men" (Luke 2:52, NIV).

It's a beautiful thing to watch our children learn. As soon as they come into the world their minds begin to absorb data like a Bounty paper towel soaks up water. By the time they can talk, they are quite willing to dispense their accumulated wisdom back to us. Sometimes the conclusions they reach leave us shaking our befuddled heads in utter amazement. Or, in the case of my friend Vern, in "udder" amazement.

One morning as she and her four-year-old granddaughter, Leslie, were having breakfast together, Vern decided to teach a few simple, straightforward facts about the milk they were drinking. Unfortunately, before the conversation ended they were both going 'round in circles, as we say in Texas. "Leslie," she began, "do you know where milk comes from?"

"Out of the carton," Leslie answered smartly.

"But," Vern continued, "before the carton . . . "

"Oh," Leslie interrupted, "it comes from the refrigerator."

"Right! But, before we get our milk from the refrigerator," Vern asked, "do you know where it comes from?"

"Sure! It comes from the store." Leslie replied with a smug look on her face.

Vern probably should have dropped the subject there, but alas, some grandmothers just don't know when they are outwitted. Pressing on, she tried to explain. "Well, before it gets to the store, milk comes from cows. Remember that cow we saw the other day? Well, all cows . . . uhhh . . . uhmmm . . . " Vern stumbled around a bit before coming up with a concept she thought her grandchild could understand. "Leslie, cows have a bag on them, and the milk comes from that bag."

Leslie's next statement made it clear this preschooler and her grandmother were not only failing to connect, they weren't even in the same pasture. "That's so funny!" Leslie giggled. "I've never seen a plastic bag on a cow."

Fortunately, as our kids mature, their level of comprehension rises and their ability to communicate improves. I've watched my grandchildren develop language skills that are nothing short of amazing. Their monosyllable utterances developed into words, then sentences that actually made sense, then into meaningful conversation. By the time they started school, I heard all sorts of wisdom issue from the mouths of our babes.

When Luke was in first grade, I joined him for lunch in the school cafeteria. Seated beside him at a table, I listened while he talked nonstop about recent events that had happened in his class. Right in the middle of a sentence, he paused, grinned at the cute little redheaded girl across from us, and said, "Well, Emma, you seem *mesmerized* by our conversation."

Now, I don't know if Luke was trying to impress his grandmother or his classmate with his language skills. But I could tell by her shy smile she was indeed "mesmerized" by Luke's command of the English language. I must admit, I was captivated myself.

Our grandchildren are not only growing intellectually, but they are also developing physically at an incredible rate. During the first year of life, our grandbabies can gain as much as half a pound per week. Thankfully, the weight gain screeches to a near halt in the second year and then continues at a measured pace until preadolescence.

When they reach the preteen growth spurt, you can see them increasing in height right before your eyes! They are not only getting bigger, but other remarkable physical changes are taking place as well. Last summer I watched Luke, twelve, morph from a cute kid into a muscular, football-toting jock in just a few short months. A transformation of this kind is wondrous for any grandmother to behold.

My friend Pat can't keep from commenting on this phenomenon whenever she sees her grandson Tim. In fact, without realizing it, she'd developed a habit of saying the same thing over and over again. (Unfortunately, I've noticed this peculiarity is not uncommon among my friends.) Recently when her family met for dinner at their favorite restaurant in Dallas, Pat burst through the door and headed toward Tim with arms outstretched. Before her mouth could form her usual "Why, you've grown at least two inches since the last time I saw you!" Tim threw up his hand and wisely prevented his grandmother from embarrassing herself in front of "The Fam."

"Don't even go there!" he quipped.

In addition to their remarkable physical changes, our grandkids are developing astute social skills. According to the experts, our kids' socialization begins sometime in their third year. And this socialization "does not necessarily start out in the world. The first steps happen in the home."[1] They are watching as their parents and grandparents interact and are coming to their own conclusions about how relationships work. Sometimes their understanding of family dynamics makes members of the older generation just a bit uncomfortable.

Such was my experience one day when I took Luke and Connor shopping to purchase a gift for their new little sister, Mary

Catherine. My hubby, Joe, and son Jason were waiting for us at the hospital with the proud parents. As we exited the department store laden with packages, three-year-old Connor was jabbering excitedly about the new baby. Somehow he slipped his hand from mine and jumped off the curb just as a car careened around the corner and headed toward us.

I was scared silly.

I grabbed his arm, spun him around, and said firmly, "Connor, don't pull away from me. You hold my hand and be careful. That car almost hit you!"

Connor was flustered. He grabbed my hand, ducked his head, and shuffled across the parking lot toward my car. As I opened the car's door, I heard him muttering under his breath, "You're not the boss of me! You're the boss of Jason and Papa Joe."

On the way back to the hospital I found myself giggling as I realized this precocious kid had already figured out "Who's the Boss" at Grandma's house. (In self-defense, it's really just a personality thing with Joe and me. I'm innately a take-charge person and, thankfully, he is a laid-back sort of guy.)

Most of us have also noticed our children becoming wise spiritually—they are growing "in favor with God." It is easy for children to believe Jesus loves them, and they readily *receive* Jesus' love and want to be friends with Him. Children are also deep thinkers and capable of great faith. Religious scholars claim, "There can be great wisdom in the simplicity of a child's understanding of the 'deep things of God.'"[2] I have to agree! At times, my grandchildren seem keenly aware of God's presence, and they are learning to relate to Him as a real person. What could be "deeper" than that?

Luke was only four when our son Matt decided he had reached a new level in his spiritual growth. Previously Luke had said memorized prayers at bedtime, and it was now time for him to learn to speak from his heart.

"Luke," Matt explained, "you can say anything you want to say to God. He is your friend. Why don't you just talk to him the same way you talk to me or to one of your friends?"

Luke quickly understood the concept. As he and his dad knelt beside the bed together, Luke uttered a few brief requests and then concluded his prayer warmly, "Good-bye Jesus. Have a nice day!"

You know, when it comes to making spiritual progress, I think it's time for us to put aside our complicated attempts to mature and follow the advice of my friend Becky: "Most of us have spent a lifetime growing up. How'd you like to join me for a bit of growing down?"[3] Who knows? If we keep heading in the right direction we just might reach kid-level and really know the "deep things of God."

✹✹✹✹✹✹

Sometimes I wonder what Mary and Joseph felt as they parented the perfect child. Did they ever feel overwhelmed by the responsibility? I wonder if His mother ever forgot, for just a minute, that her son was God. Maybe she tried to teach her omniscient child a few basics about life on this planet: "Jesus, do you know where milk comes from?" I wonder about Jesus' grandparents. Did the buttons on their robes pop when His insights wowed the religious leaders? Did they brag about how tall He'd grown?

I would like to know more about Jesus' relational style, His personality type, His sense of humor. And, to be honest, I think I'd like to debate a few issues with the all-knowing God-Child. When it comes to understanding some of the mysteries of the universe, I'm still on the same level as my preschool grandson. Oh, I understand why some things cost more than one dollar, and I've even learned to handle traffic. But, it seems to me God could have *at least* made everything fat free!

> Those who are wise will shine like the brightness of
> the heavens. (Daniel 12:3, NIV)

On Grandma's Lap

▶ When your grandchild is on your lap, ask these questions: What are things you can do now that you couldn't do a year ago? What had to happen for you to be able to do these things? What are other ways you've changed in the past year?

▶ Children, even preschoolers, need contact with peers and adults outside the family. Help your grandchildren increase their repertoire of relationships by planning a picnic, party, or social event that includes other families or groups of friends.

▶ Take a picture of your grandchild with the same prop every year. A good time to do this might be on his birthday or the first day of school. Perhaps the first and second year the child could be sitting in a rocking chair. The next year he could be standing beside the chair and a few years later, holding the chair in his hand or lifting it over his head.

▶ Mark your grandchild's height on a chart or even on a door frame. Do this regularly to show how much she has grown. I know of one family whose door frame became so important to them that they replaced the board and took the old one with them when they moved to another house.

Grandma's Tips

LEAD YOUR GRANDKIDS ON A WISDOM SEARCH

Bible scholars agree that King Solomon was the wisest man who ever lived. He was known for his pithy sayings — over three thousand of them. Some of his thoughts are recorded in the Old Testament book of Proverbs. By leading your grandchildren through this collection of sage advice, you will help them become wise men and women. Help them do a "wisdom search" by locating and listing the verses that compare or contrast the following topics. Writing the verses exactly as they appear in their Bible will help your grandchildren remember the concepts. Have them record their findings in a notebook or journal.

What are the benefits of pursuing wisdom and the consequences of folly?

- ► Describe a wise man and a foolish man.
- ► What are the advantages and disadvantages of being rich and being poor?
- ► What is the importance of honesty versus lying?
- ► Contrast life-giving words and destructive words.
- ► Describe good friends and improper friends.
- ► Compare righteousness and wickedness.
- ► List the things that are "an abomination" to God.

▶ What does Proverbs say about giving?

▶ What are the things that God considers "better"?

TIMELESS TRUTH

We actually know very little about the childhood of Jesus. The story of His growing-up years is told in sketchy bits and pieces, providing only a glimpse of what His boyhood was like. Nevertheless, the few stories we *do* have provide grandmothers with inspiration and encouragement.

Jesus is our model, not only as the perfect man showing us how to live God-pleasing lives as adults, but also as the perfect child teaching us what to expect as our children and grandchildren mature intellectually, physically, and socially.

The following verses are from the gospel of Luke:

• "When the eighth day arrived, the day of circumcision, the child was named Jesus, the name given by the angel before he was conceived" (2:21). Before their birth we look forward to our grandchildren's arrival. Usually we know them by name even before it's recorded on their birth certificate.

• "Then when the days stipulated by Moses for purification were complete, they took him up to Jerusalem to offer him to God as commanded in God's Law" (2:22). Most of us celebrate a time of dedication when our grandbabies are presented to God and their parents commit to raise them in the "nurture and admonition of the Lord." At this time we, along with other members of the church, promise to pray for them and to provide spiritual training and instruction.

- "The child grew strong in body and wise in spirit. And the grace of God was on him" (2:40). As we pray for our grandchildren and they're exposed to the truth, they'll grow not only physically but spiritually as well. We will see evidence of God's grace upon their lives.

- "Every year Jesus' parents traveled to Jerusalem for the Feast of Passover" (2:41).When our grandchildren are young, it's up to their parents and previous generations to provide spiritual training and exposure to the fundamentals of the faith.

- "When he was twelve years old, they went up as they always did for the Feast. When it was over and they left for home, the child Jesus stayed behind in Jerusalem, but his parents didn't know it. Thinking he was somewhere in the company of pilgrims, they journeyed for a whole day and then began looking for him among relatives and neighbors. When they didn't find him, they went back to Jerusalem looking for him" (2:42-45). Inevitably the time comes when children need their parents less and want to be involved in other relationships. Don't be surprised when your little ones sprout spiritual wings and begin to fly on their own.

- "The next day they found him in the Temple seated among the teachers, listening to them and asking questions. The teachers were all quite taken with him, impressed with the sharpness of his answers. But his parents were not impressed; they were upset and hurt. His mother said, 'Young man, why have you done this to us? Your father and I have been half out of our minds looking for you'" (2:46-48). Everyone, sooner or later, must examine the reality of his or her faith. As our grandchildren mature spiritually, they may have lots of questions and enjoy debating issues. At times, they may put more stock in what the teachers say than in what family members try to communicate. Don't be hurt by these outside explorations. Give the children room to examine their beliefs and come to their own conclusions.

- "He said, 'Why were you looking for me? Didn't you know that I had to be here, dealing with the things of my Father?'" (2:49). As children mature, they become sensitive to God's voice and are able to receive directions for life directly from Him. Maturity means relating to God one-on-one—like a child relates to his father.

- "But they had no idea what he was talking about" (2:50). Sometimes, just like Mary, we won't have a clue what the children are thinking and may doubt the conclusions they reach. It's all a part of healthy spiritual growth.

- "So he went back to Nazareth with them, and lived obediently with them. His mother held these things dearly, deep within herself" (2:51). When spiritual maturity occurs, our hearts will be blessed and encouraged. As our children grow, we will see changes in their attitude and behavior.

- "And Jesus matured, growing up in both body and spirit, blessed by both God and people" (2:52). God is always working in His children's hearts—revealing truth, directing decisions, dispensing grace, demonstrating love. Our little ones will mature, step-by-step, because of His faithfulness.

- "After all the people were baptized, Jesus was baptized. As he
  was praying, the sky opened up and the Holy Spirit, like a dove
  descending, came down on him. And along with the Spirit, a
  voice: 'You are my Son, chosen and marked by my love, pride
  of my life'" (3:21-22). When a child believes in Jesus Christ,
  he or she should be baptized following the example He set.
  Baptism symbolizes the death, burial, and resurrection of
  Christ, as well as the believer's "death" to a futile way of living
  and "resurrection" into a new, different lifestyle. The Holy
  Spirit's presence in the lives of your offspring proves they are
  accepted by God—chosen and marked by His love.

Small Talk with Wee Ones

You spend the first two years teaching
your children how to walk and talk,
and the next sixteen years telling
them to sit down and be quiet.

UNKNOWN

JUST THE other day my friend Becky was browsing through the
bookstore and came across a book that underscores the need for
better communicators in our world: *If Men Could Talk*. She couldn't
wait to call and tell me about it. Now, Becky and I are not into male
bashing—*definitely not!* Nevertheless, I have to admit we giggled
shamelessly before launching into deep conversation about why
such an allegation is often true. Men who can talk are certainly not
the norm these days.

In contrast to what's normal or expected in our society, I am the
mother of three men who *can* talk. Why, I've been talking to them
(and they've been talking back) since they were toddlers. Even now,
conversations between my sons and me are frequent, meaningful,

and fun. It's a skill I hope to pass on to the next generation of Malones. As I've reflected on how the men in our family developed this ability, I've come up with a few simple techniques that may help other grandmothers connect with their grandkids.

The first hurdle we have to overcome is managing our schedules to include time for relaxing conversation with those we love. Balancing life's demands is a universal problem, even for grandparents. Instead of "retiring," some grandmas have reinvented themselves as social butterflies and find their schedules filled with brunches, shopping excursions, and club meetings. Then they're surprised at how quickly the days go by, leaving little or no time for meaningful interaction with their families. Yet, in the midst of the hubbub is the nagging realization that they are missing something really important.

When my grandkids are visiting, I look for opportunities to "hang out" with them, even if it's only for a few minutes. It doesn't take much time to put my arm around their shoulders and observe their current model-building project or settle beside them on the sofa to watch an inning of a baseball game or part of a movie. When I make myself available, I often find that they open up and talk about things that are important to them, such as problems they're having with friends or some of the challenges they face in school. This is how intimacy develops. As an added bonus, I hear some of the funniest stories I'll ever hear—tales that will get passed down from one generation to the next.

One afternoon I was determined to take a little time out for meaningful interaction with our four-year-old grandson, Connor. I enticed him to sit beside me on the patio by offering him a box of apple juice and a couple of cookies. After a few moments, I asked him a question that members of my generation ask young ones all the time.

"Connor," I probed, "have you thought about what you want to be when you grow up?"

He gazed at the clouds and seemed to be deep in thought. Then he turned to me and said, "Grandma Gracie, when I grow up I want to be a horse."

A horse! Not a horseback rider. Not a cowboy. But a horse! I stifled a giggle, knowing such an irreverent reaction would end our serious conversation. Instead I cupped my hand under my chin, Freudian style, and reflected back his words. "Hmmm, a horse, huh?"

"Yep! A horse." There was no word of explanation—just a simple declaration that left me scratching my head. Then he jumped down from his chair and ran toward the swing in our big oak tree.

Later that night as I settled in my bed, my mind returned to the conversation with Connor as I wondered what in the world he was thinking. Then I got a visual picture of a sleek, black stallion running through flowered meadows—muscles rippling, breezes blowing through his mane. I pictured him grazing in lush, green pastures, drinking from cool mountain streams. As I drifted off to sleep, I decided Connor had a darn good idea.

There are some days I would gladly trade places with a horse.

Once we grandmas have figured out how to fit meaningful moments into the filled-to-the-brim days of our lives, we need to develop a few simple skills to get the conversation flowing. One of the best ways, even with preschoolers, is by asking questions. It's always best to ask those that can't be answered with a simple yes or no.

I remember one time when our grandson Luke was four. I pulled him onto my lap and jump-started the conversation by asking, "What's the best movie you've seen lately?"

Luke's voice took on a passionate tone as he answered, "Oh, Grandma Gracie, I saw *The Lion King.*"

While I was still wondering why the movie sparked such a warm response, he said something folks in our family still laugh about: "And guess what, Grandma Gracie—I didn't have to go to the bathroom one time, not one time!"

Ah, I thought, *this is a little boy's definition of a really good day.*

Being a good communicator involves a whole lot more than talking. As strange as it may seem, the best quality is the ability to be quiet—to simply listen. In fact, experts say skillful communicators spend 70 percent of their time listening and only 30 percent talking. It's a truth taught in Scripture as well. Remember reading that we're to be "quick to listen, slow to speak" (James 1:19, NIV)? Our natural response is just the opposite. Now, I know it's hard for grandmothers to be quiet when we have accumulated such a vast store of wisdom, but when we listen, we're apt to learn some amazing things from our fascinating grandkids.

For example, one Christmas, right smack in the middle of opening our gifts, my five-year-old granddaughter, Mary Catherine, cocked her pretty head to one side and sighed. "I don't know how a girl can have a baby when she's not married," she said.

It was a simple observation—one I didn't really want to address at the moment. After all, a girl's sex education is important and no grandma wants to complicate or confuse the issue. So instead of trying to formulate a response, I decided to wait and listen (and hope one of her parents might come to my rescue). As I fiddled with the ribbon on an unopened gift, it was eight-year-old Connor who finally spoke up.

"Oh, Mary," he began in a confident tone, "don't you know anything?" Then he twisted his lips into a crooked, know-it-all smirk and added, "You adopt!"

Mary Catherine seemed totally satisfied with that answer. I was delighted to sidestep that issue and get on with dispensing a few more gifts.

When grandmas are trying to connect with their grandkids, it's important to remember not to talk down to them or use too much baby talk. In fact, I like to stretch their little minds a bit by using words that make them stop and think.

Such a situation occurred recently when our grandchildren Montana, six, and Myles, three, came for an overnight visit. They'd no sooner settled in the guest room than Montana wanted to read a book to me, one he'd checked out of the library at his school. He did a splendid job reading it! In fact, when he put the book down, I raved about his expertise with phonics. "Montana," I began, "you are a great reader! Why, you pronounced every single word exactly right." Then, without even thinking about it, I used a word that caused Montana more than a little consternation: "Why, I'll bet you're the *valedictorian* of your class."

For a few moments, the little guy beamed as he basked in the glow of my compliment, but then a bewildered look crossed his face. I waited silently as the wheels of his brain seemed to be spinning out of control. Finally he spoke. "Well, Grandma Gracie, I don't know about that!" Then he shrugged his shoulders and added, "But I am the only one in my class who wears his hair spiked."

It seems to me that Montana is well on his way to becoming a "man who can talk." He's already mastered at least one good communication skill: If you don't know what the other person is saying, switch to a subject you know something about. And believe me, being cool—including sporting the latest, cool hairstyle—is one subject Montana knows something about!

After Montana and Myles had been with us for two whole days and Joe and I had just about reached our physical and emotional limits, we had an experience that perfectly illustrates my final communication principal. It comes straight from the Bible, where we are told to "speak the truth in love" (see Ephesians 4:15, NIV). When our grandchildren know we really love them —unconditionally—they will listen when we "speak the truth" about sensitive issues. And if our grandkids know they can talk to us openly, even when they have differences of opinion, sometimes they will risk saying what they really think.

Early Saturday morning, I had stumbled into the living room and was vegging on the couch, sipping coffee from my favorite mug, when little Myles darted from the guest room and cut through the dining room on his way to the kitchen. I could hear him opening the pantry and rattling through the shelves looking for something to eat. After a few minutes he strolled through the living room with a marshmallow in each hand.

Now, I admit a kid shouldn't have marshmallows for breakfast, but if I acknowledged what was going on, I'd have to get off my tush, pour a bowl of cereal, and fill a sippy-cup with milk. At that moment, that was more than I could handle.

Joe, on the other hand, became concerned about the kid's nutritional needs. As Myles continued to make runs to the pantry, I felt Joe's frustration level rising. He headed into the kitchen just in time to catch the marshmallow bandit white-handed (and sticky-handed!). "Myles," Joe bellowed, "no more marshmallows!"

Myles, who had never heard his Papa Joe raise his voice, couldn't believe what was happening. He clapped his hands over his ears—still gripping two gooey marshmallows, mind you—and ran lickety-split to the guest room, where he ducked behind the bed.

Montana, who'd been watching this drama unfold, decided to "speak the truth in love." He looked Papa Joe right in the eye, shook his head disgustedly, and declared, "I've got to tell somebody about this!"

And, that's exactly what he did.

He marched into the living room and settled on the couch next to me. Then, while his Papa Joe watched from the kitchen door, he tattled. "Grandma Gracie, Papa Joe is not handling this right!"

A few days later, after the kids were safely at home with their parents, we received a phone call from our daughter-in-law. Apparently Montana had told on his Papa Joe again—this time to somebody who would do something about it!

Jeanna asked to speak to Joe. "I'm wondering," she began in a dramatic tone, "if you can help me understand a sudden change in Myles' behavior?" She cleared her throat and continued. "Every time I offer him a marshmallow, he runs and hides in the corner."

Joe was still fumbling for words when Jeanna burst out laughing. Then, as I looked on, Joe's frown turned into a sadistic smirk and he handed the phone to me.

"As for you, Grandma Gracie," Jeanna chirped, "where were you while the marshmallow wars were going on?"

"Well," I stammered, "I'd only had one cup of coffee, and . . . and . . . "

"And what?" Jeanna asked expectantly.

My mind was spinning crazily until I remembered a tactic Montana taught me. "Well, Jeanna," I took a deep breath and continued confidently, "I can't remember exactly what happened that day, but you know what? I need a new hairstyle. I think I'll wear it spiked!"

> When words are many, sin is not absent, but he who
> holds his tongue is wise. (Proverbs 10:19, NIV)

ON GRANDMA'S LAP

Sometimes grandmothers focus on their grandchildren's physical needs more than their emotional and spiritual ones. We make sure they have enough to eat, maybe even insist they clean their plate at mealtimes. But we neglect to feed their spirit by withholding liberal doses of positive reinforcement. Next time you are with your grandchildren, try distributing a few of the following "spiritual vitamins."

10 VITAMINS FOR THE SOUL

▶ Attention—"Your smile is contagious." "I like having lunch with you."

▶ Approval—"You are beautiful!" "You have great talents." "I am proud of you."

▶ Appreciation—"You did a good job!" "That was very helpful."

▶ Consideration — "What would you like to do?" "Do you prefer blue?" "Are you tired?"

▶ Acceptance — "You are made in God's image." "I like what you did."

▶ Regard — "You are important to me." "What you said will make a difference."

▶ Kindness — "That was extraordinary." "How did that make you feel?"

▶ Gratitude — "Thank you for helping me." "You made a good choice."

▶ Commitment — "I will never leave you." "You can call me anytime."

▶ Love — "You are very special." "I love you."

Grandma's Tips

HOW TO JUMP-START A CONVERSATION

▶ What do you want to be when you grow up?

▶ What happened at school today?

▶ Have you seen a good movie lately? What's the latest book you've read?

▶ Who is your best friend?

▶ How do you feel?

▶ What are your dreams?

▶ What are your needs?

▶ What do you think about . . . ? (Insert a belief or value, current event, political situation, etc.)

▶ Say that again; I don't think I understand.

HOW TO SHORT-CIRCUIT A CONVERSATION

▶ That's the dumbest thing I've ever heard! (not respecting a child's opinions)

▶ Don't bother me; I'm busy. (having an improper concept of what's important)

▶ Don't say "funnest"! You mean more fun. (correcting grammar instead of focusing on the content of a conversation)

▶ Don't fidget when you talk. Sit still! (being impatient; interrupting; not listening to what's being said)

▶ Don't talk about your friends that way! (not allowing a chance to explain)

▶ You shouldn't feel that way. Don't be angry. Don't cry. (not validating feelings)

▶ You will never be able to play basketball! (responding improperly; missing the point; being critical instead of sympathetic)

TIMELESS TRUTH

The following verses provide principles to help us become better communicators:

• "Watch the way you talk. Let nothing foul or dirty come out of your mouth. Say only what helps, each word a gift" (Ephesians 4:29). Foul means "unwholesome," "putrid," or "rotten." Rotten words are critical, destructive, and harmful. Instead of using foul or dirty words, we are to engage in conversation that is helpful, that builds others up.

• "Make a clean break with all cutting, backbiting, profane talk. Be gentle with one another, sensitive" (Ephesians 4:31). We must avoid nagging, making sarcastic comments, or using slander. Instead, we are to be gentle and kind.

- "Forgive one another as quickly and thoroughly as God in Christ forgave you" (Ephesians 4:32). In any relationship, there are always opportunities to forgive.

- "Go ahead and be angry. You do well to be angry—but don't use your anger as fuel for revenge. And don't stay angry. Don't go to bed angry" (Ephesians 4:26). Anger is a legitimate emotion and shouldn't be squelched or denied. Suppressing anger leads to serious emotional problems, including depression. Deal with anger quickly—before bedtime.

- "God wants us to grow up, to know the whole truth and tell it in love—like Christ in everything" (Ephesians 4:15). Be truthful—not only concerning facts but also about inward qualities such as knowing who you are and not living in denial.

- "Then you will experience for yourselves the truth, and the truth will free you" (John 8:32). It is only truth that sets a person free. Jesus said, "I am the way and the truth and the life" (John 14:6, NIV). When we know Jesus, we know truth. And He will lead us into truth. "When the Friend comes, the Spirit of the Truth, he will take you by the hand and guide you into all the truth there is" (John 16:13).

- "Though some tongues just love the taste of gossip, Christians have better uses for language than that. Don't talk dirty or silly. That kind of talk doesn't fit our style. Thanksgiving is our dialect" (Ephesians 5:4). It's simple! Gossip, cursing, and coarse talking have no part in the lives of those who want to be good conversationalists.

- "Don't let yourselves get taken in by religious smooth talk. God gets furious with people who are full of religious sales talk but want nothing to do with him" (Ephesians 5:6). Don't be hypocritical about who you really are. And don't be deceived by smooth talkers.

- "He who answers before listening—that is his folly and his shame" (Proverbs 18:13, NIV). Practice being a good listener. Don't interrupt or finish another person's sentences, even in your thoughts. Be patient. Listen to the feelings behind the words. Reflect the words back. Don't jump in with words of wisdom or a solution before you have really heard what's being said.

- "Lead with your ears, follow up with your tongue, and let anger straggle along in the rear. God's righteousness doesn't grow from human anger. So throw all spoiled virtue and cancerous evil in the garbage. In simple humility, let our gardener, God, landscape you with the Word, making a salvation-garden of your life" (James 1:19-21). Listen first, speak next, then deal with anger.

- "A gentle answer turns away wrath, but a harsh word stirs up anger" (Proverbs 15:1, NIV). When someone else is angry, respond with a gentle answer instead of returning anger in kind.

- "He who conceals his sins does not prosper, but whoever confesses and renounces them finds mercy" (Proverbs 28:13, NIV). Don't try to cover up or dismiss your part of the problem. Everything needs to be on the table before a resolution can be found.

Grandparenting Is Not for Wimps

Raising kids is like being pecked to death by a chicken.
—KITCHEN PLAQUE

I REMEMBER when my children were preschoolers how much I needed a vacation—and I don't mean a trip to Disneyland. I needed some adult "time out" with people who could wipe their own noses, cut up their own food, and speak in full sentences. My friend Judy and I had a long talk about such matters one day as we walked in the woods near her house. Neither of us had parents who could (or would) take on the job of watching our kids, even for a weekend. So, Judy and I made a resolution then and there: When our children had kids and needed a break, we would be there for them. We would not become wimps!

One day, decades later, our son Matt phoned home. "Mom, we need to get away. We've planned a trip to Bar Harbor, Maine, and, well, I'm wondering if you could keep our kids for a few days?" Now

I ask you, how could I, gracious grandmother that I am, say no?

Their brood consisted of three little chicks—Luke, six; Connor, four; and Mary Catherine, fifteen months. As the appointed time of departure neared, I thought about the cute antics of my grandsons and the charming smile of my granddaughter. I could hardly wait to get those kids on my lap. I envisioned sunny days filled with warm hugs and sticky kisses, and evenings of storytelling with squeaky-clean, pajama-clad kids sitting in rapt attention.

This would be like a vacation for me too, I thought. Five days away from my usual routine, just playing with the grandkids. But when I arrived at their house, it didn't take five minutes for me to realize this trip would be no vacation! And I definitely would not be bored.

After I deposited my luggage in the guest room, I looked over the kids' schedules—complicated plans printed on an official-looking calendar with maps and a time chart attached. Their activities included three car pools, two soccer practices, and two soccer games. For the first time since I'd signed up for this tour of duty, I felt apprehensive. Later, as I watched those precious children scuffling on the living room floor, I felt weak in the knees and wondered, *Can I really do all this?*

Early the next morning, their parents flew the coop, the chicks hopped out of their nest, and the funny farm began. During the following days I mastered some coping skills, which I now offer to fellow grandparents with my blessing.

My first suggestion is to *Just Say Yes!* It's a grandparent's right! There are many times when we grown-ups must say no. After all, when we've been left in charge, we don't want our children coming home to a sick or bandaged baby. But there are other times when we almost automatically say no, when yes would work equally well. For example, one sugar-loaded jolt of caffeine will do no permanent damage to a kid, especially if he or she is getting ready to play in a large, open field. On Tuesday evening, I had my first opportunity to *just say yes.*

Luke had soccer practice at 5:30. We scarfed down TV dinners, gathered Luke's gear—shorts, shirt, shoes, socks, shin guards, and ball—and were heading for the door when suddenly he bellowed, "Wait, I need to take some water!"

No problem! I knew exactly where to find his water bottle. Mary Catherine had removed it from the cabinet at least a dozen times throughout the day, and I had put it back inside. I fumbled through the shelves, but the water bottle was not there.

"Where's Luke's water bottle?" I yelled. Luke and Connor shrugged their shoulders and helplessly turned their palms up. Mary Catherine grinned. Then Luke seized the opportunity to get something he really wanted.

With a voice as smooth as chocolate milk, he asked, "Grandma Gracie, since grandmothers are supposed to *spoil* their grandchildren, may I take a Coke?"

I stood speechless for a moment or two thinking, *This kid is really slick!* Then I answered, "Sure, grab one for everybody!" Three happy kids and one gullible grandma flew out the door and made it to soccer practice just in time.

My second suggestion is to *Take Vitamins.* When a fifty-something woman has sole responsibility for a gaggle of grandkids, physical challenges are inevitable. Hence, a handful of mega-vitamins taken at the beginning of each day is strongly advised. I found my physical elasticity stretched to the limit on Wednesday evening when our son phoned home with what sounded like a simple request: "Mom, I need my identification badge. Would you send it by overnight mail?"

"Sure," I answered. "No problem!"

The next morning after Luke left for school, I found Matt's badge, put it in an envelope, helped Connor buckle up in the back-seat of the car, buckled Mary Catherine in her car seat, loaded the stroller in the trunk, and backed out of the driveway, wondering, *Now which direction should I go?*

After twenty minutes, I located the post office, parked the car, and started unloading. Connor helped me get the stroller and unfolded it while I unbuckled Mary Catherine from the car seat. I secured her in the stroller, took Connor's hand, and managed to get them lined up inside. After ten minutes of waiting, I learned that Bar Harbor is off the U.S. post office's beaten path, so their "overnight" mail would not, technically speaking, be delivered overnight. I shoved the envelope back in my purse and headed for the door.

Back outside, I reversed the process I had just completed: unstrapped the baby, lifted her out of the stroller, buckled her snugly in the car seat, helped Connor buckle up, folded the stroller, loaded it back in the car, and decided to drive to Federal Express where overnight means overnight. Surely things would move quickly in a place with "Express" on the door.

Once there, I decided to forego the stroller. Hoisting Mary Catherine onto my hip, I grabbed Connor's hand and trudged inside. I plopped Mary Catherine on the counter and began filling out the required forms. She grabbed my pencil. When I moved her little dimpled hand, she crumpled the papers. Clearly this situation called for a change in strategy. So I put Mary Catherine on the floor next to Connor and pinned her against the counter with my legs.

"What's your return address?" the clerk asked. For the life of me, at that particular senior moment, I could *not* remember my son's address. "How 'bout the phone number?" she continued. Noticing my blank look, she shuffled through a drawer and handed me the telephone directory. But before I could even find the right page, the clerk shook her head and announced, "Lady, your baby is walking out the door!"

I whirled and ran. As soon as Mary Catherine stepped through the open door and onto the sidewalk, I swooped her into my arms like a hawk snatching a runaway chick. Mary Catherine grinned. Obviously, I would need that stroller after all.

With Connor in tow, I went back to the car, unfolded the stroller, secured the baby on board, marched back into the office, and finished the paperwork. Then I loaded the kids, drove home, put my feet up, and downed another handful of vitamins along with two Extra-Strength Migraine Excedrin.

In addition to the physical challenges we grandparents face when we interact with our progeny, there are mental and emotional frustrations as well. Hence my third suggestion—which, alas, I learned the hard way: *Never Argue with a Six-Year-Old!* It takes a determined decision on our parts, since we older folk have so much wisdom and practical information to offer. But we must remember the value of allowing those precious little ones to fail. Besides that, it feels so good to have them eventually admit that you were right after all.

It was Saturday morning when I made the mistake of trying to match wits with Luke, a kid who had just started first grade. How naïve of me! His soccer game was scheduled on field #6, something I knew for sure because his mother had carefully pointed out that the kids would *not* be playing on their usual field. If only she'd explained this to Luke.

In the parking lot, before I could even begin the interminable unfolding of the stroller, Luke surveyed the various playing fields and loudly pronounced, "Grandma Gracie, this is the wrong field."

"The schedule listed field #6," I answered confidently as I fastened the stroller's safety belt securely around Mary Catherine's tummy and grabbed Connor's hand.

"But we always play on *that* field!" he said, pointing toward one on the other side of the road.

"Well, today it's #6." Then, just to silence all argument, I added, "Your mother said so."

But Luke would not give up that easily. He countered, "My *coach* said field #5."

My feathers bristled. "Luke, you're wrong. Now let's get to field #6!"

As we trudged across the parking lot, I overheard him grumble, "Well, I believe my coach!"

Now, I'm ashamed to admit this, but I couldn't stifle a very childish comeback: "Well, *I* believe your *mother*!" I took a deep breath and pushed the heavily loaded stroller uphill toward my choice of playing field. Luke tagged along behind.

When we rounded the corner, Luke spotted his teammates on field #6—just as I had said. Before he darted onto the field, I got down on his level, and I don't mean just physically. We faced off nose-to-nose like two preschoolers tugging on one lollipop. I was right, dad-gum it, and I wanted him to admit it! After a few moments of awkward silence, I draped my arm around his shoulders, looked directly into his eyes, and asked, "Luke, were you wrong?"

He shifted uncomfortably, kicked the dirt, and answered, "I think my *coach* was wrong."

With that, I was ready to concede defeat. But I'd no sooner turned around than I felt a tug on my sleeve. As I turned back, I looked into Luke's doe-brown eyes, pooling with tears, and heard his sweet voice saying, "I'm sorry, Grandma Gracie."

Looking at his face, all my frustration vanished. We grinned at each other as I patted him on the back. Then I watched him take his place on the field, his cleats kicking up little clouds of dust. *This kid's more than smooth,* I thought. *He's absolutely charming and totally irresistible.*

Even though we grandparents adore our little ones and think their antics are precious, we must admit we need divine help to deal with them. This brings me to my fourth, and most important, grandparenting tip: *Realize You Can't Do It Alone.*

Each evening, I bathed the kids and dressed them in soft, footed pajamas. Then we huddled on the bottom bunk in their bedroom for stories, hugs, and prayers.

Before "lights out" on our last night together, Luke quoted the verses I'd been helping him memorize from the Lord's Prayer. He folded his hands under his chin and began in a reverent tone, "Our Father, which art in heaven, hallowed be Thy name. . . . " As he spoke the familiar words, it seemed to me that our heavenly Father was listening nearby.

I whispered, "Lord, You are my daily source of strength and wisdom. Thank you for being faithful." Just as I prayed for His guidance as a mother, I sought it even more as a grandmother.

When Luke finished his prayer, Mary Catherine jabbered hers, and Connor added, "God bless Grandma Gracie." I belted out a loud and heartfelt "Amen!" Tucking the covers under their chins, I kissed my grandchildren good night and cherished the priceless moments together.

The next morning, when our son and daughter-in-law returned home, I welcomed them enthusiastically with a renewed sense of appreciation. (And, I might add, a new understanding of my parents' decision *not* to keep grandchildren overnight!) "Thanks for all you do for these wonderful grandkids!" I said sincerely.

Then, in what may have been a moment of temporary insanity, I recalled my vow of yesteryear and added cheerfully, "Hey, next time you need help, just call Grandma!" With that, I packed up my vitamins, BENGAY ointment, and heating pad, then kissed my grandkids, waved good-bye, winced, and wobbled my way out the door.[1]

> Strengthen the hands that are weak and the knees
> that are feeble, and make straight paths for your
> feet. (Hebrews 12:12-13, NASB)

ON GRANDMA'S LAP

► When you are making plans to spend a night or two with your grandchildren, clear your schedule of all other activities. The children will need your undivided attention, and besides that, you will have very little energy left over for other pursuits.

▶ Your grandchildren's sports and other activities are very important to them. Whether they live far away and you are visiting them or they live close by, make plans to attend at least some of their soccer games, ballet recitals, gymnastic exhibitions, band concerts, or football games. They will be so proud to have their grandparents rooting for them from the stands. And don't forget to sneak in a hug afterward.

▶ If you spend the night with your grandchildren, don't be tempted to use the TV as a babysitter. Turn it off and read to your grandchildren. Read the classic children's stories — *The Little Engine That Could, The Ugly Duckling, Boxcar Children, Mary Poppins,* and *Pippi Longstocking.* Read Bible stories from an easy-to-understand Bible storybook. Don't forget to read poetry to them. Most children love the rhythm and fun of verse.

▶ Help your grandchildren memorize the Lord's Prayer. You will find it in the New Testament book of Matthew, chapter 6, verses 9-13.

Grandma's Tips

SAFETY TIPS FOR BUSY GRANDMAS

▶ Always buckle the children in their car seats. Don't even go on a quick trip to the corner store without buckling up.

▶ Use a stroller when shopping. It may prevent your precious grandchild from getting lost, or worse, from being abducted, and it's also easier on your back. In the grocery store, use a shopping cart with seat belts.

▶ Hold the children's hands in public, and don't take your eyes off them. They can get away quickly and become lost.

▶ Childproof your house when your grandkids come over, especially when they are toddlers. Put away breakables as well as items that might cause injury or harm. You shouldn't expect your grandchildren to leave things alone. Children are innately curious and bright. Exploring and examining things is part of their mental development and growth.

▶ Pray for your grandchildren's safety.

TIMELESS TRUTH

Being able to spend an extended period of time with our grandchildren is both a blessing and a challenge. And the challenges come on all fronts—physical, emotional, and spiritual. Before undertaking such a task (and yes, we do need to accept the challenge occasionally), we should make some preparations and adjustments. I've discovered the job is easier if I am rested beforehand, put all expectations and personal interests aside, and focus entirely on the task. You know how unpredictable kids can be, and caring for them is a full-time job—especially for those of us who are just a wee bit less energetic and agile than the kids' mom and dad.

Thankfully, into our human weakness God comes, providing everything we need to accomplish even such a daunting task as an extended child care session. We can count on the following provisions, promised to us in the Bible.

WHAT GRANDMOTHERS NEED

- Patience—"We continue to shout our praise even when we're hemmed in with troubles, because we know how troubles can develop passionate patience in us, and how that patience in turn forges the tempered steel of virtue, keeping us alert for whatever God will do next. In alert expectancy such as this, we're never left feeling shortchanged. Quite the contrary—we can't round up enough containers to hold everything God generously pours into our lives through the Holy Spirit" (Romans 5:3-5).

- Strength—"We pray that you'll have the strength to stick it out over the long haul—not the grim strength of gritting your teeth but the glory-strength God gives. It is strength that endures the unendurable and spills over into joy, thanking the Father who makes us strong enough to take part in everything bright and beautiful that he has for us" (Colossians 1:11-12).

- Love, Joy, Peace—"But what happens when we live God's way? He brings gifts into our lives, much the same way that fruit appears in an orchard—things like affection for others, exuberance about life, serenity. We develop a willingness to stick with things, a sense of compassion in the heart, and a conviction that a basic holiness permeates things and people. We find ourselves involved in loyal commitments, not needing to force our way in life, able to marshal and direct our energies wisely" (Galatians 5:22-23).

- Wisdom—"Let the peace of Christ keep you in tune with each other, in step with each other. None of this going off and doing your own thing. And cultivate thankfulness. Let the Word of Christ—the Message—have the run of the house. Give it plenty of room in your lives. Instruct and direct one another using good common sense. And sing, sing your hearts out to God! Let every detail in your lives—words, actions, whatever—be done in the name of the Master, Jesus, thanking God the Father every step of the way" (Colossians 3:16-17).

- Freedom from anxiety—"Don't fret or worry. Instead of worrying, pray. Let petitions and praises shape your worries into prayers, letting God know your concerns. Before you know it, a sense of God's wholeness, everything coming together for good, will come and settle you down. It's wonderful what happens when Christ displaces worry at the center of your life" (Philippians 4:4-7).

- Generosity — "I'd be most happy to empty my pockets, even mortgage my life, for your good" (2 Corinthians 12:15). "Put yourself aside, and help others get ahead. Don't be obsessed with getting your own advantage. Forget yourselves long enough to lend a helping hand" (Philippians 2:4).

- Faith—"How bold and free we then become in his presence, freely asking according to his will, sure that he's listening. And if we're confident that he's listening, we know that what we've asked for is as good as ours" (1 John 5:14-15).

Beyond Dr. Spock

Grandchildren are God's reward for not killing your kids.
—UNKNOWN

WHEN IT comes to child discipline, behold, one greater than Spock has come. My daughter-in-law Jeanna is knee-deep in a modern concept called "Redirecting Children's Behavior." It's all about a softer, gentler style of mothering—one that focuses on showing respect for the child and communicating without being negative. Gone are the days when a mother can tell her kids to do something "because I said so."

If you raised your kids in the 1960s or '70s, like I did, you probably did so in deference to the "spare the rod, spoil the child" principle. The paddle was "in"—at least in most church-sponsored circles. So as a young mother, I swatted my children's dimpled little hands and spanked their well-padded bottoms. When they became older, my husband and I attended a week-long seminar that taught us how to resolve the inevitable conflicts of youth. There we learned how to spank more effectively—before they got bigger than us. We literally trained our kids with a paddle in one hand and a Bible in the other.

Parents of our generation also knew how to redirect a kid's behavior; we just had other names for it. We put our toddlers in the corner, set a timer to motivate our preschoolers, and grounded our teens. *But we also spanked.* In fact, what was considered good Christian parenting then might be considered child abuse today.

Even though the discipline styles of the new millennium make me shake my graying head in amazement, I'm glad Jeanna is taking her role seriously as she mothers my precious grandsons, two-year-old Myles and five-year-old Montana. And even though we don't always agree on the *way* she handles the kids (and even though I could quote a verse or two from the Bible to back up my child-rearing theories), she has gained my approval and support.

Do we grandparents really have a better choice? It seems to me that we can either accept and support our kids or we can oppose, give unsolicited advice, and thus strain the relationship between us. While we may disagree about the methods of child training, we can always find common ground when we focus on the underlying principles that span all generations—unconditional love, consistent limits, and lots of prayer. Sometimes the most helpful thing we can do is simply relax, enjoy our grandkids, and be there when our children ask for help.

Besides that, I think it's every mother's right to parent her offspring the best way she can, using the techniques that seem to work. And no matter which formula is followed, kids usually grow up with their own unique strengths *and* weaknesses and are able to function and *dysfunction* quite well. In fact, the other day I told Jeanna, "Honey, just do the best you can. You have as much right to mess up your kids as I did when I was messing up mine."

Recently when I visited Jeanna and Mike at their home in The Woodlands, I saw their parenting style in action. I'd scarcely unpacked my suitcases when Jeanna suggested we freshen up and go out to eat. Standing in the doorway of the bathroom, I watched the following discipline drama unfold. While Jeanna patiently brushed Montana's teeth at the sink, Myles spun the roller and watched toilet paper pile on the bathroom floor. Jeanna responded to this troublesome situation with an unemotional, noncritical assertion, being careful to use "I" statements rather than "you" accusations: "Myles, *I* am not willing for *my* toilet paper to be piled on the floor."

Little Myles grinned impishly and continued spinning and piling. "Myles," Jeanna continued, "you need to rethink your decision." Myles looked at the huge mound of paper and giggled out loud as he gave the roller another twirl. Jeanna gently took the child by his hand and led him to his room. "Myles," she suggested calmly, "I think spending time in your quieting room will help you make the right choice." Then she closed the door and headed back to the bathroom to finish Montana's tooth-brushing routine.

After a few minutes, I heard the door open and glanced up to see Myles toddling toward us, arms outstretched for a hug. Since he seemed repentant and not at all interested in spinning the roller anymore, I had no choice but to accept that this redirecting stuff really works—at least with a sensitive, easy-to-manage child like Myles. But I also had to admit, it seemed much more complicated than the "just say no" method we used when our sons were growing up.

We grandparents need to remember that raising kids is *not* an exact science. Our children slipped into the parenting role, just as we did, with very little preparation and lots of uncertainty. After our little ones were born, we spent the next twenty years experimenting with whatever child-training theories were in vogue at the time. Why, in our thirty years of child rearing, Joe and I must have applied every method known in Christendom. Thankfully, God's grace covers many a parenting mistake, then and now.

A few weeks after my visit at the grandkids' house, we had a perfect opportunity to compare our different parenting styles. The family had gathered on our turf for the Thanksgiving holidays.

After dinner, I decided to check my e-mail messages. Myles followed closely behind me. When I sat down at the computer, he toddled toward my desk, zeroed in on the tiny power button, and with one chubby little finger managed to shut down the whole system. Then he turned to my fax machine, picked up the receiver, and started jabbering into the mouthpiece. Without even considering what my reaction would do to his delicate psyche, I yelled, "No, Myles! Don't play with the fax machine."

I'd scarcely got the "N" word out of my mouth when Myles looked at me as if I had kicked him in his two front teeth. His eyes filled with tears and he dropped his head on my desk and wept as if his little heart would break.

I looked to Jeanna for help, but she simply shook her head and directed an accusation toward me, something completely out of character for a woman trained in positive reinforcement techniques. She said, "Bad Grandmother!"

"But you're not supposed to make accusations!" I declared.

Then I stuck out my bottom lip and confessed, "I'm feeling really insecure right now."

Turning back to Myles, I pasted a Cheshire-cat grin on my face and purred, "Myles, *I* am not willing for *my* fax machine to be . . . " Before I could even finish my sentence, little Myles, his sagging self-confidence completely restored, looked up and grinned. Resolving to get the hang of "redirecting," I decided to share another of my nifty new toys with my grandson instead—a pop-up Scotch Tape dispenser.

I popped one of the tape strips from the gadget, pasted it on a piece of paper, and held it up for Myles to see. He turned away from the fax machine and ran for my desk, giggling out loud as he climbed into my swivel chair. He plucked one of the two-inch strips from the dispenser and stuck it on top of my desk. He reached for another and plastered it next to the first. By the time I'd rebooted my computer and gotten back online, he had created a railroad track on the desktop and was driving a choo-choo-train of paper clips down the tracks.

Later, as I fumbled through the desk drawer for a pencil, I found that Myles had wrapped a strip of tape around each of my giant-sized, vinyl-coated paper clips. Needless to say, the tape dispenser was completely empty. *Oh well,* I thought, *small price to pay for an emotionally healthy grandchild.*

Throughout their visit, I was amazed at the response of my grandchildren to their parents' new approach. The atmosphere in our home was warm, congenial, and just plain fun. In fact, Jeanna only slipped back to the '60s one time. She had watched patiently as Montana and Myles scuffled on the floor until little

Myles got pinned underneath a huge pillow. "Montana, stop it!" she yelled. "Your little brother can't breathe!" Montana could feel his mother's internal engines revving up, so he jumped to his feet and threw up his arms like a traffic cop trying to halt a speeding car. "Mom," he yelled, "don't forget about your parenting class!"

The next day, Mike, Jeanna, Montana, and Myles packed their suitcases, toys, and leftover Thanksgiving turkey into their car and headed back home. That evening, as I settled between the warm blankets on my bed, I thought about my daughter-in-law's parenting methods and about how our heavenly Father "redirects" His children—gently guiding them along dark pathways and rearranging circumstances so their lives fit into His plans.

God respects His children. He teaches them right from wrong, gives them freedom to make their own choices, and allows them to experience the consequences of their behavior. When He trains His little ones, He takes into account their own natural inclinations, interests, gifts, and talents. He opens doors and closes doors. When His kids fail, God delights in extending grace.

As I considered all this, I realized how Christlike my kids' parenting style really is. In honest reflection, I decided if I had a chance to redo my child-rearing years, I think I'd spank less and redirect more. Old dog that I may be, I am pleased to discover I am still able to learn some new child-training tricks.

However, I have to confess I'm delighted that it's Jeanna's turn to figure out how to parent perfectly and that I can just continue to be hopelessly out-of-date, but well-loved and teachable, Grandma Gracie.

Train up a child in the way he should go (and in
keeping with his individual gift or bent), and when he
is old he will not depart from it. (Proverbs 22:6, AMP)

ON GRANDMA'S LAP

► Be on the lookout for teachable moments. These special times
will probably occur when you least expect it—when you are
playing with your grandchildren on the floor or walking together
around the block. Seize the opportunity. Listen to them.
Answer their questions. Simply tell them what you know (or
don't know) about the subject. Your interest, as well as the
information you give them, will make a lasting impression.

► Look for ways to help your grandchildren discover and develop
their unique talents and God-given abilities. If they have an
interest in music, art, technology, or gymnastics, encourage
them to take lessons or attend a special class so they can excel
in that area. Enjoy the individuality of each grandchild. Don't
expect them all to be alike. Talk to each of them about their
uniqueness. Tell them how special they are to you.

► Grandparents should support the discipline style of the parents.
If your grandchildren complain about the rules or the measures
of discipline used, listen, but don't "side" with them until
you've heard the parents' point of view. Hear the children out.
Then, if there are matters that need to be addressed, talk to
the parents privately. This may take discernment to know if
there is a real problem or if the children are simply trying to
build a stockpile of grown-ups on their side. Pray for wisdom.

Grandma's Tips

THESE ARE A FEW OF OUR FAVORITE BOOKS

Jeanna's Favorites:

Redirecting Children's Behavior by Kathryn J. Kvols

Raising Your Spirited Child: A Guide for Parents Whose Child Is More Intense, Sensitive, Perceptive, Persistent, and Energetic by Mary Sheedy Kurcinka

How to Talk So Kids Will Listen & Listen So Kids Will Talk by Adele Faber and Elaine Mazlish

Gracie's Favorites:

Boundaries with Kids by Henry Cloud, John Townsend, and Lisa Guest

How to Really Love Your Child by Dr. Ross Campbell

The New Hide or Seek and *The New Dare to Discipline* by Dr. James C. Dobson

She's Gonna Blow: Real Help for Moms Dealing with Anger by Julie Ann Barnhill

---

TIMELESS TRUTH

Most grandparents are troubled by the different parenting styles of their children, especially when it comes to the "spank or not to spank" decision. Our adult children who were paddled while they were growing up often decide to adopt a more lenient style. Those who were raised by more permissive parents are prone to provide more structure in their homes—setting firmer limits and enforcing them.

Like a pendulum, methods of child discipline seem to swing from one extreme to the other with each succeeding generation. As grandparents, we can only hope our children find some middle ground. We can help them discover solutions that really work by centering our opinions and advice upon the following truths:

"Don't exasperate your children by coming down hard on them. Take them by the hand and lead them in the way of the Master" (Ephesians 6:4). To "exasperate" our children means to provoke, to overcorrect, or to make it difficult for them to obey. "Take them by the hand and lead them" indicates that our handling of children should have a certain gentleness. Children are easily discouraged when parents are too strict and overbearing. Lighten up and enjoy the children—remember how Jesus gathered the little ones around Him, how He showed genuine love and respect for them.

"Parents, don't come down too hard on your children or you'll crush their spirits" (Colossians 3:21). It is possible to "crush their spirits" if parents come down too hard on children. Crushing their spirit means treating them so severely that they become discouraged or "lose heart" (NASB). Parents and grandparents "come down too hard" on children by:

- Expecting adult behavior from them
- Criticizing when kids don't measure up to adult expectations
- Embarrassing them, teasing, or making fun of their appearance or ability
- Correcting them in public or in the presence of other family members
- Disciplining them in anger

To those prone to react in anger, author Julie Ann Barnhill offers some practical advice:

> Sometimes you can short circuit a volcanic explosion by concentrating on your physical reactions. Remind yourself to breathe deeply and slowly, concentrating on the flow of air in and out of your lungs. Consciously relax your facial muscles—unclench your jaw and teeth, raise your eyebrows to smooth out your forehead, unpurse your mouth. Deliberately stretch out your hands (which may be clenched into fists) and roll your shoulders to relax your neck. By changing your physical response to anger, you may be able to cool down your emotional response as well.[1]

In certain situations, parents and grandparents are prone to come down too hard on the children:

- When trying to impress somebody who has more compliant or "perfectly behaved" children
- When taking them into an adult situation and having unrealistic expectations
- When expecting them to sit still or pay attention longer than their short attention span allows
- When pushing them beyond their physical limitations, forgetting that children have boundless energy, need to eat more frequently, and go to the restroom more often

These situations, which may seem like minor annoyances to adults, are likely to crush the spirit of a child because:

- They are demoralized and devalued
- They lose their sense of self, their feeling of well-being
- They feel rejected and unloved
- They experience frustration—wanting to please but repeatedly falling short

Parents and grandparents can prevent some of these uncomfortable situations from happening by:

- Establishing clear guidelines beforehand so the child will know what's expected
- Making allowances for the child's immaturity—physically, emotionally, and spiritually
- Setting consistent limits and using consistent discipline

"He who spares the rod hates his son, but he who loves him is careful to discipline him" (Proverbs 13:24, NIV). The "rod" is a symbol of authority. The Hebrew word can be used to denote a scepter, a walking stick, or a weapon. In the Psalms, the "rod" is a shepherd's crook and is used to guide and rescue a straying lamb. The shepherd didn't strike his sheep with the rod. David said the Lord, the Good Shepherd, has a "rod and a staff" that "comfort" the sheep.[2] The "rod" is also used to chasten an errant child of God.[3] At times, God used calamity as a "rod" to correct the behavior of His people.[4] To "spare the rod" means neglecting to provide guidance, failing to administer discipline, or undermining authority by removing or protecting the child from the consequences of his or her choices.

Parents or grandparents "spare the rod" when they:

- Act as if the offense didn't really happen
- Lie about or fail to reveal the offense
- Make excuses to the person in authority about why the offense occurred
- Take the child's punishment for him, bail him out, or cover for him

"Train up a child in the way he should go (and in keeping with his individual gift or bent), and when he is old he will not depart from it" (Proverbs 22:6, AMP). Training a child "in the way he should go" means:

- Training should consider each child as an individual. Every child is unique and different, not only in physical features but also in personality, skills, and interests. To try to make any child a cookie-cutter image of another is not only wrong but also impossible.
- Training should take into account each child's own personal "bent"—his or her natural inclinations and interests.
- Training indicates having a plan that includes instruction, guidance, and support. To train requires time and effort.
- When we train our children with their particular "bent" in mind, they will not depart from this training when they get older, for they will have realized their purpose and found their true self.

It's About Time

Once over the hill, you pick up speed.
—CHARLES M. SCHULZ

MY LIFE has not become less complicated now that I am a member of AARP. In fact, I'm busier than ever. I still have all the same interests I had when I was thirty-something, and on top of that, I have a bigger family. In addition, I've been hit hard by the reality that time moves faster on the other side of midlife. I'm literally over the hill and on a roll, albeit gathering no moss along the way! Nevertheless, I'm determined not to allow the tyranny of the urgent to crowd out things that are really important in life—such as taking a walk with my grandchildren.

❄❄❄❄❄❄❄

One Sunday afternoon early in February, my hubby and I decided to visit our son and daughter-in-law and their blended family of six children. We'd scarcely parked and begun climbing out of our car when the door swung open and three pixie-like granddaughters ran down the sidewalk to greet us. As soon as they ushered us inside, they began pulling on their sweaters and shoes, hopping from one foot to the other as they tried to straighten their socks and fasten the Velcro straps. In a chorus of excited voices, they suggested, "Let's go for a walk in the forest! Grandma Gracie, will you and Papa Joe take us for a walk?"

I grinned as I thought about the "forest" behind their house. To me it looked like an overgrown, neglected piece of property, but to the girls the huge oak trees and winding trails had all the enchantment of Pooh Bear's Hundred Acre Wood.

Now, I must admit, when faced with the choice of hiking through the woods with the girls or sprawling on the sofa in our son's living room, my first reaction was to say no and sink into the plush cushions. But the excited look on the faces of my granddaughters convinced me to go for the adventure. I grabbed a sweater and took Mary Catherine by the hand. Abby linked hands with Papa Joe, and Ingrid ran alongside. Joe and I were pulled out the door toward the path behind their house that led down the hill and into the woods.

Apparently the girls were quite familiar with their "forest," for once we lost sight of the house, Mary Catherine assumed the role of guide, directing us along the trail while shouting instructions over her shoulder: "This is the way. Watch out for the briars! Be careful crossing the ditch."

When we reached a steep incline, Abby took hold of my hand to steady my steps as I shuffled down one side and climbed up the other. "Be careful, Grandma Gracie," she coaxed, "the path is steep." Then she reached for Joe's hand, saying, "Watch your step, Papa Joe, I don't want you to fall." It was sweet to see this youngster taking care of us.

We followed the girls up one hill and down another, around a dry creek bed, and past a concrete dam with a pool of water. On the other side of the creek stood the remains of an old stone house—a few stacked bricks and cinder blocks, a stone fireplace, and in the backyard, an old barbecue pit made of rocks and mortar with a rusted grill on top. We circled the area and headed on toward a small pond surrounded by willows and cattails.

On the far side of the pond, a fallen tree made a crude bridge over the shallow water. There must have been a dozen turtles basking in the sunshine, lined up on the tree trunk like a bunch of kids waiting for a ticket to the water park.

"Look at the turtles!" Mary yelled. "It's a turtle traffic jam!" The noise must have startled the creatures, for one by one they plopped into the pond, making a loud *kerplunk* as their hard shells hit the water.

Once the turtles had vacated their place in the sun, the girls started chucking rocks into the pond. Joe searched the ground for a few smooth, flat stones. Then he demonstrated his skill at skipping them across the water's surface, making a series of circular ripples. As the girls watched their Papa Joe, their upturned faces conveyed a sense of deep satisfaction. Being in their own Enchanted Forest and having the undivided attention of their grandparents made the girls feel totally happy. Being with those you love in a quiet, restful place is enough to satisfy any human heart—grandmothers included. Why, even turtles like to congregate in the woods with a few kindred spirits.

After a few more minutes, the girls were ready to head back home.

Ingrid and Mary Catherine led the way, while Abby kept a close eye on her grandparents. When we reached the remains of the old stone house, I spotted a fallen tree near the path—a natural bench for weary travelers. As I sat down on the trunk, I pulled Abby onto my lap and asked, "Abby, I wonder who lived in that old house. What kind of family do you think lived there?"

Abby's eyes popped with excitement as her imagination kicked into high gear. "I know, I know!" she said. She took on a theatrical stance. Using dramatic hand gestures and animated facial expressions, she launched into a story. "Once upon a time, a long time ago, a daddy and a mommy and two children lived in the little house. One was a boy and one was a girl."

I smiled as Abby cocked her head to one side and appeared to be deep in thought. "And one day a storm came. . . . " She paused and sucked in a gulp of air. "And a big wind blew a tree down on top of the house, and the family ran and ran and ran—all the way to California!"

While I was still picturing the little family hotfooting it all the way from Texas to the West Coast, Abby pulled me to my feet and started running ahead down the pathway toward home. (I couldn't help but make a mental note as we headed down the path: That girl just may be the next Jan Karon.) "Come on, Grandma Gracie!" Abby yelled. "Hurry, Papa Joe! It's time to go home."

As we struggled down the steep bank of the dry creek and scrambled up the other side, I thought about how special this time had been. Because we'd taken time to walk with them through the woods, our precious granddaughters knew, in a fresh way, that they were important to us. That day, we didn't have to *tell* them we loved them. Our jaunt through the words spoke louder than any words we could have said.

When we reached our son's back door, I checked my watch. We had been gone only thirty minutes, but the experience we'd shared with our granddaughters had created memories that will last a lifetime.

※※※※※※

When Joe and I were raising our kids, the emphasis in Christian circles was on spending "quality time" with your kids. "When it comes to finding time for your children," child-rearing pundits declared, "it's not *quantity* but *quality* that counts." This philosophy confused me. When I was too busy, I thought, *Oh well, even if I haven't spent much time with my children today, tomorrow I'll take them to the park for some real quality time. Quality will make up for the lack of quantity.* On the other hand, when I did have a more relaxed schedule including time with my family, my mind was all awhirl as I wondered, *Now, how can I make this time meaningful?*

Eventually I adopted a different motto: *To a child, love is spelled T-I-M-E.* I can identify with this saying—to a wife, a parent, a friend, or a grandchild, love is spelled exactly the same way. When we really care about a person, we'll find a way to spend time with them. (Remember when you were dating?) I quit beating myself up for not spending enough time (can it ever really be enough?), and I gave up analyzing every moment to see if it was meaningful. I was able to relax and *enjoy* my children. Today I realize that having a relationship with my grandchildren requires T-I-M-E, and I simply look for opportunities to be with them and make the most of the opportunities I do have.[1]

For most of us, putting family first requires decisive planning. I write the appointments with my grandchildren in my calendar—and I write in ink. For I know unless I make definite plans, my time will be swallowed up by the busyness of everyday life. Even with strategic planning, sometimes my plans go awry. When that happens, I've learned to be flexible, to accept the fact that God is in control of my life—even which friend meets me for lunch or which grandchild I take shopping. I make plans, but I also realize that God is in charge. "In his heart a man plans his course," Scripture declares, "but the LORD determines his steps" (Proverbs 16:9, NIV).

One Saturday morning when Luke, six, and Connor, four, had come for an overnight visit, Joe and I decided to take them on a nature walk. By the time the boys filled two canteens with water and packed a few survival rations into a backpack, the hot Texas sun was beaming overhead. Nevertheless, we pulled on loose clothing, donned our sunglasses and baseball caps, and struck out down the country lane. After a few minutes, Joe directed us onto an abandoned dirt road. We hadn't gone far until it was time for our first of many water breaks. We looked for the nearest shade, uncapped our canteens, and broke out the snacks.

While we were sipping water and munching on raisins, Joe glanced down and saw a series of animal tracks in the sand. "Look, boys," he said, "a raccoon has been here since the last rain and left footprints." The two city slickers were quite impressed! After a few minutes, Connor noticed some smaller tracks, and Luke concluded that a whole family of raccoons resided in the nearby grove of trees.

The boys ran into the woods in hopes of getting a glimpse of the raccoon family. (Joe looked at me and raised his eyebrows as if to say, *There's not a raccoon in Hunt County that would give an audience to this rambunctious pair!*) Eventually the boys gave up the search and jogged up and down the road looking for more tracks. Finally we reached the end of the road and circled back toward home.

A few days later when their parents returned, Luke and Connor couldn't wait to tell them about our hike. Apparently our nature walk could be classified as quality time. It made a lasting impression on our grandsons, and, to be honest, their grandparents treasure the memory as well.

A few weeks later, Joe and I decided to take a walk down the same road we'd traveled that hot, dusty day. Seeking refuge from the sun, we rested beneath the same oak tree. Then we noticed something interesting. Not only were the raccoon tracks still obvious in the dirt, but the imprints of our grandsons' tennis shoes were there too — right beside the animal tracks. As we looked at the tracks, memories of that special time with Luke and Connor took a leisurely stroll in my mind.

Later that evening as I relaxed on the redwood deck in our backyard, I was still thinking about my wonderful grandchildren and the special imprint their lives have made on my soul.

That's the way life is, isn't it? We are all making tracks in the sands of time, leaving footprints others will follow. Hopefully the imprints we make will lead our future generations along a scenic road strewn with precious memories.

> Whether you turn to the right or to the left, your
> ears will hear a voice behind you, saying, "This is

the way; walk in it." (Isaiah 30:21, NIV)

ON GRANDMA'S LAP

> Beware the barrenness of a busy life.
> —SOCRATES

▶ Somehow you must find time for a good long walk with your grandkids. The experience will be one the children will never forget—and you will have a great time yourself.

▶ Choose an interesting place to walk. Few grandparents have a nearby "Enchanted Forest," but most of us can find a park, botanical garden, or zoo.

▶ Try to find a park that has a small lake or pond. Children love water and the creatures that inhabit such a place.

▶ A simple jaunt around a neighborhood block can be a real adventure for your grandchild, especially if you are on the lookout for birds, butterflies, squirrels, dogs, and bugs.

▶ Take along your field glasses so your grandchildren can see the birds and animals up close.

▶ Buy your grandchild a disposable camera and let him or her take pictures of the flowers and interesting plants.

Grandma's Tips

T-I-M-E AND LONG-DISTANCE GRANDMOTHERS

I'm blessed to live close to my grandchildren, so I can easily spend thirty minutes walking through the woods with them, visit their schools, and attend their birthday parties. But most grandparents reside some distance from their children; some live in another state or even another country. They learn to connect with their grandkids in other creative ways. I've gleaned the following tips for long-distance grandparenting from several of my friends. May their ideas help you find T-I-M-E for your grandkids even though it comes from a distance.

▶ Mickle loves to read to her grandchildren. She's learned to "reach out and touch" them by reading books to them over the phone. She buys two copies of her favorites, keeps one, and sends the other to her grandkids. As she reads to them they can look at the pictures and turn the pages together, even though they live miles apart.

▶ Judy says, "Children love packages! I try to send one on every special occasion." When her grandchildren lived in Scotland for a few years, her grandson loved to receive packages containing his favorite foods from the United States. Judy takes each of her grandchildren to Disneyland when he or she is four years old. They spend one day at Disney, just going at their own pace, and another at the beach. Because she and her husband live in the country, they have constructed a tree house and go-cart track for their kids to enjoy when they come for a visit. All three of Judy's grandchildren like to cook, so she allows them to help her prepare their favorite dish—and she doesn't complain about the mess!

▶ Linda, who has older grandchildren, tries to stay connected via telephone and e-mail messages. She and her husband plan a special gathering once a year at an event called "Tabernacle"— an old-fashioned camp meeting that's been taking place for 176 years in West Tennessee. Their grandchildren also come to visit them in Tennessee every year for Christmas.

► Glenna and her husband, who have five granddaughters, stay in touch by making lots of visits, even flying to Phoenix or Las Vegas to see their long-distance kids. They try not to miss their special occasions—including athletics, church, and school happenings. They communicate through plenty of e-mail messages, telephone calls, and short notes. The families meet every year for family week at Glorieta Christian Conference Center.

► Ruthie invites her long-distance grandson to spend two weeks with her husband and her each summer. Because they live on Lake Granbury, it's not a bad place for a kid to spend a vacation. Their grandson also flies in for important family occasions such as weddings and family reunions. When her other grandchildren were little and lived at a distance, Ruthie liked to send comical drawings to them in the mail. Sometimes she sent a stick of gum taped to an index card.

► Gail sends her grandchildren decorations for the various holidays, such as Valentine's Day and Easter. This makes her part of the celebration even though she may not be there herself. She buys them all special pajamas to wear on Christmas Eve and gives them a Christmas ornament each year with their names and the year marked on the back. Gail and her husband, Virgil, love to fly and visit their long-distance grandkids as often as possible. They also send tickets to the children so they can fly their direction. Gail and Virgil own a beachfront condo, where the family gathers in the summer.

Timeless Truth

I keep a very detailed calendar. Even phone appointments are recorded in the tiny book I've often called "my brain." This written brain has become more important to me with each passing year, especially now that my real brain, the actual gray matter the Lord gave me, seems to have more holes than Swiss cheese.

Writing things down helps me find time for the people most important to me—my husband, an aging mother, three sons, two daughters-in-law, and eight grandchildren. Thankfully, the Word of God provides insight into how busy grandmothers can make the most of the time we have.

- Solomon muses about life and reminds us there is an appropriate time for every activity.

> There's an opportune time to do things, a right time
> for everything on the earth:
>
> A right time for birth and another for death,
> A right time to plant and another to reap,
> A right time to kill and another to heal,
> A right time to destroy and another to construct,
> A right time to cry and another to laugh,
> A right time to lament and another to cheer,
> A right time to make love and another to abstain,
> A right time to embrace and another to part,
> A right time to search and another to count your losses,
> A right time to hold on and another to let go,
> A right time to rip out and another to mend,

A right time to shut up and another to speak up,

A right time to love and another to hate,

A right time to wage war and another to make peace. . . .

God made everything beautiful in itself and in its
     time. (Ecclesiastes 3:1-8,11)

- Everybody has been given the same amount of time each day.
  Nobody gets twenty-two hours, while another gets twenty-six.
  It's what you *do* with the time that counts.

  Make the most of every chance you get. These are
  desperate times! (Ephesians 5:16)

- Taking a walk with your kids is a "biblical" thing to do. In fact
  it's assumed *we will be* walking along the road with our little
  ones alongside. (The verse says "when," not "if," you walk.)
  While doing so, use the opportunity to teach them important
  truths, those dearest to your own heart.

  Place these words on your hearts. Get them deep
  inside you. Tie them on your hands and foreheads as
  a reminder. Teach them to your children. Talk about
  them wherever you are, sitting at home or walking in
  the street. (Deuteronomy 11:18-19)

- God is walking with us wherever we go—holding our hands
  and keeping us from stumbling—not only in a physical sense,
  but spiritually as well.

  Stalwart walks in step with GOD;
      his path blazed by GOD, he's happy.

> If he stumbles, he's not down for long;
>> GOD has a grip on his hand. (Psalm 37:23-24)

- As we read and study God's Word, we'll find direction for our lives. Our steps will be confident and sure when we clearly know God's will. The Psalmist declares, "Your word is a lamp to my feet and a light for my path" (Psalm 119:105, NIV). That simply means God's Word gives us direction just like a bright flashlight illumines the pathway ahead of us so we can see which way to go.

> Steady my steps with your Word of promise.
> (Psalm 119:133)

- God expects us to make plans; it would be foolish not to. But we must remember that He is sovereign—ultimately in control of every event that happens in our lives. We make our plans, but it is He who determines whether or not those plans ever come to fruition.

> We plan the way we want to live,
>> but only GOD makes us able to live it.
> (Proverbs 16:9)

- We belong to God. Our life is not really our own to do with as we please. A popular bumper sticker reminds us, "There is one God! You are not Him!"

> I know, GOD, that mere mortals
>> can't run their own lives,
> That men and women
>> don't have what it takes to take charge of life.
> (Jeremiah 10:23)

- If the uncertainty of life makes you feel uncomfortable, take heart in knowing that whatever God promises will certainly come about. *His plans* never fail to materialize.

  > I am GOD, the only God you've had or ever will have—
  >   incomparable, irreplaceable—
  > From the very beginning
  >   telling you what the ending will be,
  > All along letting you in
  >   on what is going to happen,
  > Assuring you, "I'm in this for the long haul,
  >   I'll do exactly what I set out to do." (Isaiah 46:9-10)

- God is personally involved in the daily comings and goings of His children. He is holding us in His hands, and nothing can hurt us when we're in this safe place.

  > Hour by hour I place my days in your hand,
  >   safe from the hands out to get me. (Psalm 31:15)

- The Holy Spirit lives in our hearts, guiding our lives literally from the inside out. He nudges us to go in certain directions, stops us from taking wrong paths, and gives us insight into God's will. We don't have to plan our days with a preset agenda or follow some sort of spiritual rule book. We don't even have to agonize over which verse of Scripture contains the direction we need for today. We simply begin each day in quiet trust, listening to the "still, small voice" of God's Holy Spirit. Then keep up with Him—one step at a time.

  > Let us keep in step with the Spirit. (Galatians 5:25, NIV)

To Tell the Truth

Some of us learn from other people's mistakes;
the rest of us have to be the other people.

—BARBARA JOHNSON

AS THE story goes, an old farmer went to the city one weekend and attended the big-city church. When he came home his wife asked him how it was.

"It was good," said the farmer, "but they did something different. They sang praise choruses instead of hymns."

"Praise choruses?" asked his wife. "What are those?"

"They're sort of like hymns," the farmer said, "but they're different in some ways."

"Well," his wife persisted, "what is the difference?"

"The best way I can explain it is like this," the farmer said. "If I were to say to you, 'Martha, the cows are in the corn,' well, that would be a hymn. If, on the other hand, I said to you, 'Martha, Martha, Martha, Oh Martha, *Martha, Martha!* The cows, the big cows, the brown cows, the black cows, the white cows, the black and white cows, the cows, cows, *cows,* are in the corn, are in the corn, *are in the corn,*' well, that would be a praise chorus."

❄❄❄❄❄❄

Most members of my generation, even those who live in the big city and attend big-city churches, struggle with the new trends in worship, especially when it comes to music. We're not opposed to having a certain amount of freedom to express our feelings toward God if the praise is genuine. But we've been around long enough to know that just saying a thing doesn't make it so, even if you say it a dozen times.

Besides that, if we're really honest, we have to admit we simply don't like change. Most of us grandmothers want our children to raise our precious grandkids embracing the same traditions, along with the same moral and spiritual truths, that we ourselves have embraced. You know what I mean. We want them to be solid right-wing conservatives—and premillennial, dispensational, traditional, Baptists, Methodists, or Presbyterians—just like us.

But, alas, some of our kids develop minds of their own. Even if they stay connected to the right denomination (in our humble opinion), there's still a possibility they might go off on some spiritual tangent and become charismatic or, only slightly better, adopt a worship style that's too formal or ritualistic.

You'd think with all the weird religions and different worldviews prevalent today that I'd be happy just knowing my grandchildren believe in Jesus. But I want more than that for them. Don't you want the same for your grandchildren? I want them to have a close, intimate relationship with Christ—a relationship that has its roots growing deeply in the fertile soil of a warm, traditional church, like the one I attended when I was growing up.

Even the building of the church I attended in my formative years exuded warmth. Its tawny limestone and red brick walls framed with fresh white paint gave its exterior the appearance of a Norman Rockwell painting. Huge oak trees and well-groomed flowerbeds filled with purple and yellow pansies provided a certain homey feeling as we parked our cars out front. I always had the feeling that I was entering someplace sacred, yet full of love, as I made my way up the steep marble steps toward the ornate double doors that graced the front stoop.

Once inside the small auditorium, we were welcomed by honey-colored hardwood floors and polished oak pews with velvet cushions. The scent of lemon oil hung heavily in the air. In the center of the platform at the front, a massive oak pulpit stood like a sentinel guarding the truths contained in the huge open Bible on the communion table. In the corner was a grand piano, something I'd never seen or heard anywhere else but in my church. I'll never forget the majestic hymns the pianist played on that glorious instrument.

On Sunday mornings, seated in a pew next to my mother, I watched as the sun shone through the stained-glass windows and cast a rosy glow on our faces. Even the windows proclaimed the truths of Scripture. One of my favorites pictured Jesus as the Good Shepherd. He was surrounded by a flock of sheep and carried a lamb on his shoulders. Another window portrayed Jesus at prayer; another, Moses cradling the Ten Commandments in his arms. These images remain indelibly in my mind.

More important than the warm surroundings were the warm-hearted people who worshiped in the church of my youth—my Sunday school teacher, a deacon who always greeted me with a bright smile, and my pastor, a jovial man who reminded me of Santa Claus.

Now, I ask you, how could anyone want a church different from that?

※※※※※※

For years I waited and prayed for my adult children to find a church home—a place where our grandchildren could receive the same kind of spiritual training their parents had received. Then one day, the phone rang and my daughter-in-law Jeanna announced, "Gracie, we're gearing up our search for a church. I got on the Internet and found one I think we'll like. Want to check it out?"

Well, yeah! Of course I did. As soon as I hung up the phone, I revved up my search engine and located the one she'd mentioned. And guess what! Their mission statement was theologically correct, their doctrinal stance sound. I did, however, suspect the church was a bit on the contemporary side. My suspicions were confirmed a few days later when Jeanna called again.

"Oh, Gracie," she began in an animated tone, "our new church is *just perfect*. We felt so welcome and loved. Besides that, we felt comfortable. The pastor wore a sport shirt and khakis. His sermon only lasted about twenty minutes so the kids sat still through the whole message. The music was just great! Two screens up front displayed the words of the songs so we didn't have to use a hymnal. Instead of pews, they had plush theater seats. And besides that, they had guitars and drums and strobe lights, and . . . "

As she continued talking, I couldn't help but notice the absence of many of the traditions I held dear. I found myself thinking, *No organ, no choir, no anthems? How can a perfect church have no pews? Oh, my!*

The next day, our other daughter-in-law, Rachel, called. "Gracie, we went to a new church, and you know what?"

I was afraid to ask.

"There were so many people there," she continued, "we had to take a shuttle from the remote parking lot to the front door—you know, like the shuttles at Six Flags. They served cappuccino and donuts in the foyer. And the order of service was printed on card stock that looked like a CD cover. A big *X* was printed on the front above a picture of a guy on a skateboard. It looked like they were advertising X-treme sports or something." She laughed before adding, "I guess we attended X-treme Church!" She paused. "The sermon was really good and the kids just loved it."

As soon as I hung up the phone, I was back on the computer checking websites.

After a bit of research, I discovered both churches declared a firm belief in the foundational truths of the New Testament church—the Great Commission and the Great Commandment. (I breathed a huge sigh of relief just knowing my grandbabies would be connected with groups that stood on solid footing.)

I was very familiar with Christ's Great Commission to the church. In fact, I had memorized the verses in my Sunday school class when I was a little girl: "Go and make disciples of all nations, baptizing them in the name of the Father and of the Son and of the

Holy Spirit, and teaching them to obey everything I have commanded you" (Matthew 28:19-20, NIV).

Throughout my life I've been associated with assemblies that have followed those principles—going, baptizing, teaching, obeying. In fact, my church of choice has always been evangelical—in addition, of course, to being solid right-wing conservative, premillennial, dispensational, and traditional!

I was familiar with the Great Commandment, too. Jesus said, "'Love the Lord your God with all your heart and with all your soul and with all your mind.' This is the first and greatest commandment. And the second is like it: 'Love your neighbor as yourself'" (Matthew 22:37-39, NIV). I've known these verses for as long as I can remember, but as I thought about it, I realized that the churches of my choice did not emphasize the Great Commandment as much as the Great Commission. I wondered why.

Could it be that, with all our emphasis on correctness, we had failed to place the proper value on the most important truth of all? Have we loved God with all our heart, soul, and mind? Have we loved others as we love ourselves? I found myself wondering if, when all is said and done in this life, the final questions will be, *Have you been doctrinally sound? Have you zealously held onto tradition?* Or will they be, *Have you loved well? Have you loved God with all your heart? Have you loved your fellow man?* I was beginning to think I might have been slightly mistaken about what constitutes a "perfect church."

The next day I decided to call my friend Sam Douglass, pastor of a fast-growing church in Texas. According to Sam, he didn't set out to build the biggest church in town. His goal was simply to meet the needs of the people. It just so happened that lots of people wanted to come to a place where they felt loved.

I also found out that his church had adopted a contemporary worship style. The words of the praise choruses and hymns, as well as the points of Sam's message, are projected on a screen at the front of their auditorium. He explained, "People living in our culture today are not auditory learners. We are visual learners. When we meet together to worship, what's wrong with using visual aids to make the truth clearer, to make it stick? We project the choruses on screens so people can focus more on worshiping God and not on the hymnal."

I had to agree with Sam about one thing. Members of the younger generation are visual learners. The last time I visited my grandkids, thirteen-year-old Luke was playing a video game on his dad's computer. It was mounted in a metal frame—an engineering masterpiece that our son Matt designed and built himself—that holds three monitors, three computers, one printer, a scanner, a cable modem, a router, a fax machine, and two speakers. I could hear the faint sounds of music coming from a set of headphones hanging loosely around Luke's neck, the TV was blaring in the background, and three children were romping on the floor. To me the scene was chaotic, but Luke was focused on the screens, completely tuned in to the task at hand.

At that moment I understood why contemporary church services are so appealing to the younger members of our family. They thrive in chaos!

Later that evening as I settled beneath the warm blankets on my bed, I couldn't help but lament the way things have changed in the last few decades. And then my mind turned to a scene in the future.

I got a visual picture of myself sitting in a wheelchair with a great-grandbaby nestled on my lap. Jeanna, Rachel, and my sons were sporting gray hair and wool sweaters. And my grandchildren were talking about how special their church had been when they were growing up.

In my imagination the dialog went like this: "I just loved my church when I was a kid. The worship experience was, well, *totally awesome!* As the praise team sang and the words of the choruses flashed up front, a gal at the keyboard pounded out the melody and a guy on drums kept the tempo. I'll never forget the great music from that synthesizer!

"Thousands of people gathered every Sunday to fill the huge auditorium. Even the building was an inspiration to me. It was an architectural masterpiece with hundreds of crystal-clear, tempered glass windows set in stainless steel frames. Why, even the podium was made of clear plastic. Everything sparkled, clean and bright and cool. The fresh scent of Windex wafted through the air. . . . "

Suddenly I felt a giggle gurgling up from the depths of my soul, and it really didn't seem important anymore whether or not my children sang hymns or choruses, wore suits or khakis, clapped their hands or sat reverently, or even if the sermon was long or short. I just wanted them connected to a group of believers over-flowing with God's amazing, boundless love.

> When the Friend comes, the Spirit of the Truth, he
> will take you by the hand and guide you into all the
> truth there is. (John 16:13)

On Grandma's Lap

▶ When your grandchildren are on your lap, it's a perfect time to teach them spiritual truth. It seems they all have questions — "How big is God?" "What does eternal mean?" Answer in simple terms, giving truth appropriate for their age.

▶ Plan a "Take Your Grandchildren to Church Day." Seeing their grandparents put a high priority on church attendance will make a lasting impression on your little ones and will reinforce the spiritual training they're receiving from their parents. (My friend Fran took her granddaughter, Emily, to church one Sunday morning. As they pulled into the parking lot Emily asked, "Mimi, why are we going here today?" Fran answered, "This is where your grandpa and I worship God." The next day when they drove by the church, little Emily piped up, "There's the church where you worship God!" Fran was pleased that Emily understood this important concept.)

▶ Try memorization. It is a great way to deeply implant truths about God in a child's heart. Help them memorize a psalm, verses that meet a special need, or a verse for each letter of the alphabet. (See Appendix for a list of verses tied to the alphabet.)

▶ You may also want to help your grandchildren memorize the order of the books of the Bible so they can be more familiar with the overall content of the Bible and locate verses easily.

Grandma's Tips

Growing Little Bookworms

Because of the special bond that exists between them, grandmothers are able to influence their grandchildren in all sorts of ways. One of the most important things we can do is help them appreciate good books. Here are seven of my favorites that teach important concepts. They are also completely charming to read.

1. *You Are Special* by Max Lucado
2. *Just in Case You Ever Wonder* by Max Lucado
3. *The Topsy Turvy Kingdom* by Dottie and Josh McDowell
4. *Chattaboonga's Chilling Choice—A Story About Trusting God* by Sheila Walsh
5. *In Search of the Great White Tiger—A Story About Following God* by Sheila Walsh
6. *A Faith to Grow On—Important Things You Should Know Now That You Believe* by John MacArthur (Winner of a Gold Medallion, this book is chock-full of faith-building tips, biblical insights, and resources to keep kids growing. It includes Word Scrambles and Questions and Answers done in a colorful, kid-oriented style.)
7. *The Extreme Teen Bible* (This is an actual Bible that doesn't look like one, translated in the popular *New King James Version*. Each book has an introduction, character profiles, a Bible reading plan, 250 thought starters, and questions and answers. And it's all written in a "way cool" X-treme style that teens love.)

TIMELESS TRUTH

In the early days of church history, believers "committed themselves to the teaching of the apostles, the life together, the common meal, and the prayers" (Acts 2:42). These four areas of commitment serve as a good pattern for churches today. They can also serve as guidelines, helping us to know whether or not our children and grandchildren are connected to a good, sound group of believers.

• Are they committed to the "teaching of the apostles"?

> It was all his doing; we had nothing to do with it. He gave us a good bath, and we came out of it new people, washed inside and out by the Holy Spirit. Our Savior Jesus poured out new life so generously. God's gift has restored our relationship with him and given us back our lives. And there's more life to come—an eternity of life! You can count on this. (Titus 3:4-8)

> Is it not clear to you that to go back to that old rule-keeping, peer-pleasing religion would be an abandonment of everything personal and free in my relationship with God? I refuse to do that, to repudiate God's grace. If a living relationship with God could come by rule-keeping, then Christ died unnecessarily. (Galatians 2:21)

• Are they enjoying "the life together" with other believers? Are they part of a small group through which they can experience the blessings of true friendship and fellowship with other believers?

> Let's see how inventive we can be in encouraging love and helping out, not avoiding worshiping together as some do but spurring each other on, especially as we see the big Day approaching. (Hebrews 10:25)

> Each one should use whatever gift he has received to serve others, faithfully administering God's grace in its various forms. (1 Peter 4:10, NIV)

> He handed out gifts of apostle, prophet, evangelist, and pastor-teacher to train Christians in skilled servant work, working within Christ's body, the church, until we're all moving rhythmically and easily with each other, efficient and graceful in response to God's Son, fully mature adults, fully developed within and without, fully alive like Christ. (Ephesians 4:11-13)

- Are they committed to "the common meal"? (Early church members visited in each other's homes for meals together. Some think this refers to sharing the "Lord's Supper" or "Communion" meal.)

> They followed a daily discipline of worship in the Temple followed by meals at home, every meal a celebration, exuberant and joyful, as they praised God. (Acts 2:46-47)

> Every time you eat this bread and every time you drink this cup, you reenact in your words and actions the death of the Master. You will be drawn back to this meal again and again until the Master returns. (1 Corinthians 11:26)

- Jesus said, "My house will be a house of prayer" (Luke 19:46, NIV). Does the group encourage prayer, praise, and worship?

> When you come before God, don't turn that into a

theatrical production either. All these people making a regular show out of their prayers, hoping for stardom! Do you think God sits in a box seat? Here's what I want you to do: Find a quiet, secluded place so you won't be tempted to role-play before God. Just be there as simply and honestly as you can manage. The focus will shift from you to God, and you will begin to sense his grace. (Matthew 6:5-6)

Your worship must engage your spirit in the pursuit of truth. That's the kind of people the Father is out looking for: those who are simply and honestly *themselves* before him in their worship. God is sheer being itself—Spirit. Those who worship him must do it out of their very being, their spirits, their true selves, in adoration. (John 4:23-24)

Some grandmothers have concerns that go much deeper than which church their kids attend. They're concerned because their grandchildren don't go to church, they've joined groups that teach error, or their parents are apathetic about spiritual matters. When this is the case, grandparents are put in a precarious situation. To say nothing may mean their grandkids will grow up with distorted views of God and wrong information about how to have a relationship with Him; to speak up may jeopardize their relationship with their adult children, perhaps even closing the door on communication with the grandchildren. While we members of the older generation hesitate to interfere, we know it is only the truth that sets a person free.[1] When we speak, we must "speak the truth in love" (see Ephesians 4:15, NIV). Children and grandchildren will not be easily offended when we're careful to present the truth without undermining parental authority.

> God wants us to grow up, to know the whole truth
> and tell it in love—like Christ in everything. We take
> our lead from Christ, who is the source of everything
> we do. He keeps us in step with each other. His very
> breath and blood flow through us, nourishing us so
> that we will grow up healthy in God, robust in love.
> (Ephesians 4:15-16)

God has promised to complete what He has begun in our children. You can trust Him to love, protect, and guide them. The following verse is a good one to pray for your grandchildren. Try substituting their names in place of the pronoun "you."

> There has never been the slightest doubt in my
> mind that the God who started this great work in
> you would keep at it and bring it to a flourishing
> finish on the very day Christ Jesus appears.
> (Philippians 1:6)

Stepfamilies—All Mixed Up or Nicely Blended?

Happiness comes through doors you didn't even
know you left open.

—UNKNOWN

WHEN OUR boys were growing up, they teased Joe and me about being the prototype for the Ozzie and Harriet sitcom. And if we were Ozzie and Harriet, our two oldest sons were David and Ricky.

Our family was far from perfect, but we loved each other and knew how to settle problems with rationality and self-control. Never once did we threaten to kill the kids or divorce each other. In fact, I don't remember the "D" word ever being used in our house. We were committed and determined to stay together, to work things out.

We taught our boys that marriage is a covenant. Much more than a contract between a man and woman, it is a binding agreement among three—including God Himself. Marriage is not to be entered into lightly nor terminated easily. In addition, I did what most moms of my generation were taught to do — I started praying for our sons' mates while they were still playing little league, even during the stage when they thought all girls had germs.

Eventually they got over their aversion to the opposite sex (thank the good Lord) and started looking for Miss Right. When they finally found the gals I'd been praying for, I was thrilled. My prayers were answered. I just knew my sons would be entering into married bliss that would last a lifetime. I wasn't naïve enough to think their coexistence would be trouble free; I just figured the problems they did have would be little ones — or at least things that could be handled with customary Malone rationality and self-control.

When I first heard that our oldest son, Matt, and his wife were having serious problems, I couldn't believe it. Joe and I intervened. We listened and talked, we bought and distributed books that might help, and we helped them find a good counselor. I vacillated between prayer (believing God would perform a miracle) and crying — often in the same day. But in spite of everything, the differences between my son and his wife eventually proved "irreconcilable."

Divorce happened.

And it hurt the people I loved most, including my precious grandchildren.

Nevertheless, once the divorce was finalized, I set my heart on trying to find at least some good in the profoundly sad circumstances that threatened to engulf our family. Isn't that what we all believe? That "in all things God works for the good of those who love him" (Romans 8:28, NIV)? Does "all things" include human mistakes and failure?

Of course it does!

After a year or so, one of the good things that came about was a beautiful blue-eyed woman with long blond tresses who had grown up in France. She not only spoke French beautifully, she spoke the language of love and new life into the aching heart of our son. *C'est l'amour!* Eventually, Matt brought Rachel home to meet his folks. We were captivated by her charming personality and grace. A few months later we met her two daughters.

Ingrid, barely three, looked like a miniature version of her mom with long blond hair and blue eyes set in a pixie-like face that made me want to pick her up and give her a great big Grandma Gracie hug. But when I stretched out my arms, she ducked behind her mother's skirt, then peeped out and grinned shyly. Lexi, eight, a charming brunette with a captivating smile and gorgeous olive-toned skin, greeted us politely and also passed on a Grandma Gracie hug. I realized, then and there, if a marriage did take place in the future, it would take time for these girls to warm up to the idea of having another grandmother.

Before long, Matt and Rachel began planning a summer wedding. It would be a family affair that included Matt's four children and Rachel's two. The highlight of the ceremony for me was the lighting of the unity candle. One huge candle was placed on a table within easy reach of all six children. Matt and Rachel assisted as each child struck a long-stemmed match and touched the wick with their tiny flame. (I held my breath and, with typical grandmotherly concern, watched for stray sparks that might ignite a piece of lace or lock of hair.) The candle was lit in an almost synchronized manner as the preacher addressed the children: "Do you promise to love each other, to respect each other? And do you promise to do your part to make this family happy and successful?"

"We do!" a chorus of cheerful voices responded.

I'm sure the vow of unity made on that pivotal day has faced its challenges. But the children genuinely love each other. And they seem to like each other, too. Whenever all six gather under one roof, it's just plain fun for everybody present—including the grandparents.

As I have observed the successful blending of our son's family, I've noticed several factors that have helped bring that success, including consistent discipline and the honoring of boundaries. Of course the discipline dramas that have unfolded in my presence have been of the not-so-serious kind. For example, it's normal at our grandkids' house to have heated debates over which chair each child should occupy at dinner.

Recently, at Abby's birthday dinner, it looked like we were playing a game of musical chairs as the kids moved from one place to another, jockeying for position. Then the pushing began. "I want to sit by Grandma Gracie," Ingrid said. "No, it's my turn," Mary whined. "You sat beside her last time." (As the circling continued, I couldn't help but relish the fact that Ingrid had not only overcome her shyness around me, but she'd finally decided to call me "Grandma Gracie.") After another round or two, Connor bellowed in an authoritative tone, "Mary, why don't you just sit down!"

Then their daddy cleared his throat and gave those kids a look that stopped all arguments mid-sentence. Everybody slipped into the nearest chair and reached for his or her napkin. The scene I had just witnessed had a familiarity about it, conjuring up images of another time when our sons Matt and Mike were fussing over who would sit beside their dad or who would ride in the front seat of the car. Only in this scene, Papa Joe was the daddy doing the glaring. As I settled in my chair, I found myself thinking, *Is there a parent among us who has not mastered "the look"?* Then my wicked sense of humor kicked in and I thought, *So this is how parents get even— their children grow up and have kids of their own. Sweet revenge!*

What's a grandma to do when situations like this occur? In this case I was tempted to jump in the middle of the fray and agree with Mary. I remembered our last visit and the outcome of musical chairs on that occasion. Mary had, once again, wanted to sit by me, but Ingrid slipped behind her, plopped down in the coveted chair, and quickly took a sip of milk from the Barbie glass in front of her. She knew that once she'd actually "contaminated" the glass, the place would be firmly established as hers. I started to share my recollections with the whole group when a verse from Psalms came to mind: "Post a guard at my mouth, God, set a watch at the door of my lips" (Psalm 141:3). It seems to me, when the parents are present, keeping her mouth shut is the best course of action for a grandma to take, especially when the ruckus involves stepgrandchildren.

Grandparents face an entirely different situation when the parents are not present. In that case we must reinforce the disciplinary style of the parents and stepparents, doing what we think they would do if they were there. Unfortunately, our tendency is to let our grandkids do as they please, ignore bad behavior, and think they will love us more if we're lenient. Actually, the opposite is true. If our little ones have clear-cut boundaries that are the same whether with parents, stepparents, or grandparents, they'll be happier and better adjusted. In fact, psychologists agree that children with clearly established limits feel more loved than those without guidelines, who don't know what to expect.

Our friends Bruce and Fay are a good example of grandparents who know how to establish and enforce loving limits. They have a close relationship with their three granddaughters, Elizabeth Grace, Rebekah Faith, and Susanna Joy. (Don't you just love those names?) Since the girls spend lots of time at their grandparents' house, it's important that parental limits are reinforced when the girls are in their care. It isn't always an easy thing to do. Recently, when they took the girls to McDonalds for lunch and to play on the playground, Rebekah, almost three, got into a battle of wills with her grandpa.

When Bruce said, "It's time to go home," she didn't argue; she just sweetly ignored her grandpa's suggestion and headed back to the slide. Unfortunately for Rebekah, when she zipped off the end of the slide, she landed right in her grandpa's arms. Bruce got down on one knee so he could look his little one directly in her pretty blue eyes. (I'm sure I don't need to tell you that kneeling is not an easy thing for a grandfather to do. Nevertheless, because of his great love for this little girl, Bruce was willing to bear the pain. And, unfortunately, he would have more opportunities to suffer before this encounter was over.)

Making eye contact, Bruce said, "Rebekah, I want to remind you of one of Grandpa's rules." Rebekah shuffled her sock-covered feet and gazed over her grandpa's shoulder. Bruce pressed on. "The Grandpa rule is this: When I tell you it's time to go, I mean it's time to go. Now get your shoes and let Grandma help you put them on."

Rebekah nonchalantly turned away as if she were going to totally disregard Grandpa Rule Number One. Bruce knelt again (groan). "This is the second Grandpa rule: When I say 'get your shoes' that's exactly what you must do. This time I'll help you get them." Together they retrieved the shoes and Rebekah took them to her grandma. As soon as their little feet were properly shod, three happy girls and two exhausted grandparents made their way to the car and headed home. The girls' parents, Christopher and Julie, would have been proud of their mom and dad.

It's important for boundaries to be observed in many areas. Remember, when my daughter-in-law married Matt, she had no concept of what it's like to parent boys, especially Malone boys— guys who like compu-toys, fast engines, and weird animals.

Matt's marriage to Rachel brought about much more than a blending of two families. There's been a blending of cultures and literally a blending of two different worlds. She brought lace curtains, modern art, and French perfume into Matt's world; he brought motor oil, fast-moving vehicles, and loud music into hers. If ever there was an example of the adage "opposites attract," Matt and Rachel are it.

Nevertheless, in spite of her inexperience, Rachel has done a great job of handling our grandsons. I remember one incident that occurred recently that shows how far this stepmother is willing to go to meet the needs of her complicated family.

Thirteen-year-old Luke needed someone to care for his pet while he and his siblings vacationed in New York. Now, I have to tell you that Luke's pet is not a dog. Or a cat. Or a bird. Lizzie is a chameleon—and not your ordinary garden variety of chameleon either. Luke had carefully explained that to me earlier when he brought the reptile into the living room to meet me. "There are three different varieties of chameleons," he explained. "Lizzie's an African chameleon."

Connor piped up at that point: "She's like a miniature dinosaur."

That's exactly what she looked like. The jagged points of skin under her chin and down her spine looked prehistorical indeed. Her skin was a lovely shade of teal blue, and contrary to what you might think, soft and sleek. Her green eyelids opened and closed like the shutter on a slow-speed camera, protecting her bulging eyes from too much sunlight. She had a long tail that curled into a spiral and thin arms with tiny hands and long fingers that moved in slow motion as she crept across my lap. I had to admit, Lizzie was, well, charming.

If this get-acquainted meeting between Lizzie and me gives you the willies, just remember I grew up surrounded by boys—sister to three brothers, mother of three sons, grandmother of four grandsons. I learned long ago to deal with critters. But I do have my limits, as you will see later.

As the story goes, Luke needed a lizard-sitter and Matt had risen to the occasion, promising to provide food and water and appropriate amounts of TLC while Luke was away. But there was one hurdle yet to overcome. Matt was going out of town for three days, and Rachel would be in charge of Lizzie during that time.

I was present when the reality of that situation hit home.

As Luke and I sat at the table talking, Rachel walked in, leaned on her elbows so she could look Luke right in the eye, and said,

"Luke, we've got a problem."

Rachel took a deep breath and continued, "Looks like I will be in charge of Lizzie while Matt's gone, and I don't know the first thing about taking care of her."

"Well, first of all," Luke began, "Lizzie eats worms."

A stricken look crossed Rachel's face, and she shuddered. "Worms? What kind of worms?"

"Meal worms," Luke answered, "from the pet food store. I have some in my room, but . . . " Luke hesitated before adding, "Well, you've got to kill the worms before you give them to her."

Rachel turned white around the mouth. "Luke, that's horrible! I refuse to even touch a worm, let alone kill one. You'll have to kill a three-day supply before you go."

"But Rachel," Luke replied calmly, "Lizzie has to have fresh food. It's simple. You just hold the worm with a pair of tweezers and squash its head. Then, all you have to do is show it to Lizzie and she'll zap it right out of your hand with her long, sticky tongue."

Rachel was beside herself. *Sacré nom d'un chien!*

Luke looked over his shoulder at me, hoping I could come up with some solution. "Sorry," I muttered, "even for a nice grandkid like you, I don't think I could." However, I could sense the tension building between my daughter-in-law and grandchild, so I jumped in with an idea. "Luke, can Lizzie eat anything else? Can't you get some other kind of lizard food from the pet store—perhaps something that's already deceased? You know, Fast Food for Reptiles?"

"Grandma Gracie, don't you know anything about chameleons?" Luke thought about it. "I guess we could get some crickets. Lizzie can eat crickets while they are still alive."

Rachel and I both breathed a sigh of relief until Luke continued, "Just take the live cricket from the package, dust it with vitamin powder . . . "

Rachel held her squeamish tummy as she left the table. But eventually, after she'd had time to gather her wits about her, she came back in the room with a legal pad in her hand. It seemed to me her attitude had taken on just a touch of Malone rationality and self-control as she said, "Write it all down, in detail, step by step."

You know, as I think about all this, it kinda reminds me of an Ozzie and Harriet sitcom.

> God sets the solitary in families; He brings out those
> who are bound into prosperity. (Psalm 68:6, NKJV)

ON GRANDMA'S LAP

▶ Don't be surprised if your stepgrandchildren warm up slowly. It may take several months for them to feel comfortable on your lap or even carrying on a personal conversation. Give them plenty of time. Eventually they will respond if you resist the urge to be pushy. I'll never forget the day when all six grandchildren ran down the sidewalk to greet Papa Joe and me as we parked out front. I was thrilled when little Ingrid's voice rose above the rest as she called out, "Hi, Grandma Gracie."

▶ Purchase a small box for each child and label it with his or her name. Between visits, collect a few inexpensive gifts to place in their special boxes. These can be stored in a bookshelf or closet. My friend Fran selected a small organizer with four removable drawers. Whenever her granddaughters and stepgranddaughter come, they can't wait to see what Mimi has put in their box. The surprise gifts don't have to be big—a small flashlight, some stickers, a coloring book, new markers (the water-soluble kind), a small toy, or some special mints or gum will delight your grandchildren.

▶ Be careful to treat your stepgrandchildren and grandchildren with equal favor. Don't show partiality. Pay equal attention; give uniform gifts. Compliment them for their admirable qualities and achievements. Make them feel part of the family by attending some of their school functions, sporting events, or recitals.

Grandma's Tips

One evening I went to bed thinking about Bruce and Fay's "Grandpa Rules" and woke up wondering, *If our stepgrandchildren had the freedom to make a few rules for their stepgrandparents, what would they be?* I came up with the following list.

Stepgrandkid Rule Number 1: "Please give me time to adjust. I've been through a lot. My whole family has changed. I'm still trying to get used to having a new parent and now I find out I have another grandmother. I already have two. I think I like you, but right now it feels funny and awkward when you try to hug me."

Stepgrandkid Rule Number 2: "Please don't compare me to your other grandchildren. I am unique. I have special abilities and talents that you haven't discovered yet. Someday, when I trust you more, I'll let you see what I'm really like."

Stepgrandkid Rule Number 3: "Please don't ask me questions or make critical comments about my parents. I feel caught in the middle when you probe for information about the other side of the family."

Stepgrandkid Rule Number 4: "Please don't twist your lips funny or raise your eyebrows when I talk about my other parents or grandparents. I notice it when you do."

TIMELESS TRUTH

Feeling the pain of economic hard times, Elimelech and Naomi moved from Bethlehem to Moab with their two sons. They were sickly little boys and needed good food. It was supposed to be a temporary relocation, but the family ended up building a home and staying longer than expected. After a few years, Naomi's husband became sick and died. The grieving widow continued to live in Moab while her sons grew up and married. Then, in an unfortunate turn of events, both sons died and left Naomi brokenhearted and homesick.

She decided to go back to Bethlehem, so she gathered her belongings and consulted with her two daughters-in-law. They both wanted to go with her, but Naomi explained something she had learned from experience: It would be hard for a young widow to find happiness in a foreign land, living with strangers.

The story that follows has much to teach us about how to make relationships work well—even the complicated relationship between a mother-in-law and her daughter-in-law or between stepparents and stepgrandparents.

The drama unfolds in the Old Testament book of Ruth.

- Naomi was not afraid to admit her mistakes and failures.

  > The LORD's hand has gone out against me!
  > (Ruth 1:13, NIV)

- Naomi was unselfish, more concerned for the needs of her daughters-in-law than for her own. She accepted her daughters-in-law as her own children. She called them her "daughters."

  > After a short while on the road, Naomi told her two daughters-in-law, "Go back. Go home and live with your mothers. And may GOD treat you as graciously as you treated your deceased husbands and me. May GOD give each of you a new home and a new husband!" (Ruth 1:8-9)

- Naomi didn't hold back on giving counsel, but the final decision rested in the hands of her daughters-in-law. Naomi accepted Ruth's choice.

  > When Naomi saw that Ruth had her heart set on going with her, she gave in. And so the two of them traveled on together to Bethlehem. (Ruth 1:18-19)

- Naomi and Ruth loved each other deeply with a spiritual bond based on truth. Ruth believed in Naomi's God.

  > Don't force me to leave you; don't make me go home. Where you go, I go; and where you live, I'll live. Your people are my people, your God is my god; where you die, I'll die, and that's where I'll be buried; so

help me GOD—not even death itself is going to come
between us! (Ruth 1:16-17)

- Naomi faced reality. Even when she was overcome with anger
  and bitterness, she did not deny her feelings. Instead she freely
  expressed her pain to the God she trusted. Because she knew
  Him as the Almighty God, "The Strong One," she knew that the
  blame for her sufferings rested squarely at His door. She exem-
  plified real, gutsy faith that remained strong even as she challenged God's goodness. Ruth learned from her mother-in-law
  (even as we do today) that it's okay to be angry about death,
  divorce, or any other bad thing that happens. It's perfectly normal and healthy to express those feelings. God can handle emotional honesty!

  > The Strong One has dealt me a bitter blow. I left
  > here full of life, and GOD has brought me back with
  > nothing but the clothes on my back. Why would
  > you call me Naomi? God certainly doesn't. The
  > Strong One ruined me. (Ruth 1:21)

- Naomi was genuinely concerned about Ruth's well-being. In
  turn, when Ruth met Boaz, Naomi found hope for the future.

  > So where did you glean today? Whose field? GOD
  > bless whoever it was who took such good care of
  > you! (Ruth 2:19)

  > Why, GOD bless that man! GOD hasn't quite walked
  > out on us after all! He still loves us, in bad times as
  > well as good! (Ruth 2:20)

When Ruth and Boaz had a son, Naomi became a grandmother—actually, a *stepgrandmother*.

Theirs was a "blended" family. The union brought together two different nationalities—Hebrew and Moabite. They had to deal with two different religions—Ruth left her foreign "gods" and accepted Naomi's God. There was a cultural "blending" as well. Ruth left behind her family traditions, along with the rituals of the Moabites, and accepted the Jewish traditions of her new family. Those included the laws of Moses, particularly that of the kinsman-redeemer.

Naomi couldn't have loved her grandson more if he'd been the product of her own son. Scripture records the feelings of Naomi's friends: "Blessed be God! He didn't leave you without family to carry on your life. May this baby grow up to be famous in Israel! He'll make you young again! He'll take care of you in old age. And this daughter-in-law who has brought him into the world and loves you so much, why, she's worth more to you than seven sons!" (Ruth 4:14-15).

Deep contentment flooded Naomi's soul. She "took the baby and held him in her arms, cuddling him, cooing over him, waiting on him hand and foot. The neighborhood women started calling him 'Naomi's baby boy!' But his real name was Obed" (Ruth 4:16-17).

The story has a remarkable ending. When tiny Obed grew up, he became the grandfather of David, *an ancestor of Jesus.*

Ho-Ho-Holidays

Let's put the fun back in dysfunctional.
—MARY ENGELBREIT

SHORTLY AFTER I got married, certain realities hit hard. For one thing, I was no longer simply my mother's "baby girl" and my fella's sweetheart. I had become a daughter-in-law to my hubby's domineering mother, a sister-in-law to Joe's four siblings, and low woman on the totem pole when it came to making decisions about how to celebrate family holidays. For an up-front, take-charge (okay, bossy) woman used to having her own way, this was a major adjustment—major!

According to the Malones, Christmas just wasn't Christmas if the whole family couldn't gather on December 25. This presented a problem for my own family of origin (as they say in psychological circles). You see, my side of the family likes to celebrate Christmas, too. And it only seemed right to me that at least half the time, we should do so on Allen turf on December 25. I even came up with what I considered a creative plan: Every other year the Malones could celebrate the holiday on the Sunday *before* Christmas. But no matter how I defended my position, it seemed I could not win.

Even when I pulled out my Bible and tried to prove that Jesus wasn't even born in December, much less on the 25th, the Malone jury decided in favor of the plaintiff. The same Malone Compulsory Attendance Rule applied on Thanksgiving, and Easter, and Mother's Day, and Father's Day, and everybody's birthday. How unreasonable!

Nevertheless, I dutifully attended the events and *appeared* to be having a good time. But inside—deep in my heart where nobody else could see—I was longing to be with my own clan. I felt a lot like the little boy whose mother disciplined him regularly by sitting him in the corner. One day he just couldn't hold back a response: "I may be sitting down on the outside," he grumbled, "but inside, I'm standing up!"

Now, I'm not trying to incur your sympathy. I've matured a bit now that I'm easing into the Golden Years and have realized that the choices I made back then to join in on all the Malone family functions, regardless of my feelings, were really because of my own *dysfunctions*. At that point in my life, I preferred to please my husband and have his family think I was wonderful than to speak up and demand equal time for the more compliant Allens.

Things got better when Joe's brothers and sisters got married and had children. As the family increased, the matriarch's unrealistic expectations seemed to relax. In fact, on most occasions, so many members of the boisterous brood gathered in the Malones' tiny farmhouse that I actually think Joe's mom was relieved when there were a few no-shows.

In addition, I eventually dealt with my personal shortcomings and developed enough gumption to utter a quiet comeback to my mother-in-law's persistent invitations. The first time I said, "I'm sorry, we have other plans," I expected the earth to open up and swallow me whole. When it didn't, I grew in confidence, and we began to develop some traditions of our own. Later, as my children married and had little ones, I knew from experience that I needed to be flexible.

And so it is today. Every family celebration I organize has a Plan B.

For example, last year I had an inkling it would be difficult to gather our offspring under the same roof at the same time, so in lieu of a full-blown Christmas dinner, I opted for a Christmas buffet to be served whenever.

Before the weekend was over, we ended up having three gift-giving sessions and two Christmas buffets. And you know what? Not once during the entire time we were digging through packages and feasting on Christmas goodies did anybody even notice we were doing it at the "wrong time"!

I realize such juggling of holiday plans would give Martha Stewart the heebie-jeebies. But, I think it's better than the alternative. I'd rather celebrate an occasion with cool-headed, happy people at some offbeat time than have even one son, daughter-in-law, or grandchild feel pressured to be at Grandma's house or, worse yet, wish they could be with somebody else.

It's also comforting to know that not every Christmas will be so chaotic. In fact, next year it's Matt's turn to have his children on Christmas morning. If Mike and Jeanna follow their same pattern and Jason doesn't have a girlfriend who invites him to join her family for Christmas brunch, we all might be present on Christmas morn. But who knows what might happen by this time next year. I can only be certain about one thing—whoever shows up will have a grand time.

Unfortunately, ours is not the only family that faces problems as they make plans for the holidays. I know dozens of people who feel burdened because their parents expect them to spend every holiday trekking through packed airports or traveling hours along highways on their way to Grandma's house. It seems to me it's time for members of my generation to cut our kids some slack. Some of us need to chuck our Norman Rockwell image of Christmas, buy ourselves an airline ticket, or pile into our SUV and make our own journey "over the river and through the woods." Our children will rise up and call us blessed if we're willing to make a few concessions.

It's taken a while, but I'm learning "to be content whatever the circumstances" (Philippians 4:11, NIV). That includes large family gatherings with everyone present or small intimate groups with just a few of us. After all, each has its own unique charm.

Even during the most hectic holiday, meaningful moments have a way of transpiring. I remember one such occasion a few years ago when Montana was four—that wonderful age when children begin to think deeply and question everything. He and his parents, along with baby Myles, had arrived late, unpacked their car, and begun settling in for a long winter's nap. After Jeanna dressed the boys in their pajamas, Montana climbed in my lap to say good night. As I held him close, he noticed a brass pendant I wore on a chain around my neck. The medallion depicted the nativity scene, complete with the Holy Family and two members of the heavenly host.

As Montana fingered the shiny necklace, he began asking questions. "Grandma Gracie, who is that man standing there?"

"That's Joseph," I answered.

"Who is that girl?" he asked pointing to the tiny woman seated in the straw.

"Her name is Mary. She's the baby's mother."

"Uhmmm . . . " Montana's brow wrinkled. "And who is that teeny little baby?"

"That, my precious child, is baby Jesus, God's own Son. He came from heaven and was born in a manger."

"What's a manger? Why is the star sooo big? And . . . and . . . " He took a huge gulp of air and with eyes wide pointed to the two angels hovering near the star. "Grandma Gracie, who are those guys?"

"Oh, Montana, those are angels—two of the *strongest dudes* in God's army. They came to tell the shepherds about the baby and to watch over Him while He was sleeping."

Montana responded with a simple, "Oh!" and slid off my lap. Our conversation had ended, but I would never forget the imprint it made on my heart. The old, old story had taken on a new freshness. I choked down a lump in my throat as I realized that in that unplanned moment, Montana and I had rediscovered the true meaning of the season. Later I realized that such a meaningful exchange would not have happened if I'd been grumpy because my children had arrived later than I had planned.

Christmas is not the only occasion when I've had to be flexible.

As important as my grandchildren's birthdays are to me, I usually don't get to celebrate the occasion with them in person. I talk with them by phone on their special day, and I send the out-of-town kids a package. When we're able to arrange a party with those who live nearby, it's almost always on what the Mad Hatter refers to as an "un-birthday." It wouldn't be my first choice, but we've learned that "un-birthdays" can be just as much fun as real birthdays—if everybody brings a good attitude to the party.

Last year when Mary Catherine turned seven, we finally gathered our brood to celebrate her birthday two weeks after the actual event. She was beside herself with the anticipation of having our undivided attention on the day we had chosen. Matt reported that she landed at his house on Friday evening wearing a giddy grin and immediately began plying him with questions: "Daddy, are we gonna have my birthday party tomorrow?"

"We sure are!" Matt assured her.

"Well, are we going to have my favorite foods?"

"You bet!"

"Okay!" she chirped. Then she took a deep breath and began, "For breakfast . . . "

Matt stifled a chuckle as Mary Catherine laid out the menu for the *entire day*. "For breakfast I want pancakes—no, I mean waffles. You know, the little round ones with square holes. You know how the syrup fills up all those holes? Yep, I want waffles!"

"Yes, honey, I know."

"And for lunch, I want macaroni and cheese. For dinner I want chicken—cooked on the grill."

When Matt told me about this conversation, I thought, *That girl knows what she wants and goes after it.* It never even crossed Mary's mind that we might *not* want to spend the entire day adoring her while feasting on her favorite foods.

We've also learned not to have unrealistic expectations concerning Mother's Day and Father's Day. After all, my daughters-in-law have mothers and fathers, too. Some of our grandchildren have stepmoms and stepdads as well. In addition, most of them have grandmothers and even great-grandmothers they want to remember. When you consider all these family members, I'm surprised (and pleased) when I receive a special card or a bouquet of flowers. I've learned to appreciate whatever expression of love comes my way. Sometimes, an over-the-top celebration occurs. I'll never forget the Mother's Day party my kids arranged last year.

Joe and I had dinner with Matt and all six grandkids on Saturday evening—not on the traditional Mother's Day, mind you, but the night before. After a luscious meal, the kids presented me with a beautiful leather-bound journal. And, best of all, everyone had written a personal message inside.

"Read it out loud, Grandma Gracie," a chorus of voices urged as I pushed back the brightly decorated bag and crumpled tissue and opened the book.

The first message was from my daughter-in-law Rachel. *You have lived with a man who is obsessive about his toys, and you raised three of the most complicated, interesting, difficult boys I know—and you have survived! This gives me inspiration. For this reason and many others, I love having you for my mother-in-law.*

Following her entry, five-year-old Ingrid had carefully printed in bold letters, *Happy Mother's Day Grandma Gracie.*

Connor had issued a to-the-point one-liner: *I love you because you're you.*

On Mary's page, she wrote eloquently in her best cursive style, *You are so very nice to us whenever we visit. Now it is our turn to do it for you because it is Mother's Day.* She completed her entry with a bit of artwork—a stick-figure grandmother wearing a big smile (I love it when someone draws me skinny) and a caricature of herself presenting a gift of great monetary worth. I knew this for sure because the present was marked with big dollar signs on all four corners. In the bubble above the grandma's head were the words, *Oh, this is so nice!* and the little girl quite nicely replied in return, *Thank you.*

Lexi wrote in a bit more formal style: *I love you lots. I'll miss seeing you today because I'm going on a road trip. I hope this letter will take my place. So, this is my message, Happy Mother's Day.*

On the next page, four-year-old Abby surprised me with her printing ability. Knowing my "Abbs" as I do, I figure she dictated the message to one of her siblings and then painstakingly copied every letter. The words were quite legible: *Dear Grandma Gracie, I love you. Abby.*

I turned the page and began reading the literary tome that thirteen-year-old Luke had written. It began, *Grandmothers are mothers who are grand. Restoring the sense that our most precious things are those that do not change much over time. No love of children is more sublime, demanding little, giving much on demand, more inclined than most to grant the wings on which we fly off to enchanted lands. . . .*

By the time I'd reached this point, I knew something was up, for the kids sitting around the table were snickering and covering their mouths with their hands. As I read on, some of them began laughing out loud, slapping their knees, and hanging on to their chairs. Nevertheless, I continued reading in a serious tone, *Though grandmothers must sometimes serve as mothers, helping out or maybe taking over, each has all the patience wisdom brings, remembering our passions more than others, singing childish songs we long remember.* By the time I reached the salutation—*Happy Mother's Day, I love you*—even Luke was laughing uncontrollably. Eventually he gained his composure and confessed, "I got it off the Internet."

Connor shrugged and fessed up as well: "I did, too!" He grinned as he added, "But I really meant it."

The final entry in my journal was written by Matt. *Wow,* he began, *either the writing gene has been passed on to another generation, or I've raised a bunch of plagiarists. Happy Mother's Day from all of us. They meant every stolen word. I love you.*

Now, I ask you, is there a grandmother among us who would *not* be delighted with such a gift?

❊❊❊❊❊❊

I realize that our family celebrates most holidays out of sync with the rest of the world. But at least we keep in step with our own needs and wants. You may think we've sacrificed a lot, but it seems to me we've gained much more than we've lost. We respect each other, and our nontraditional celebrations overflow with grace and love. If you doubt it, let me remind you that my grandchildren spent hours traversing the World Wide Web to find appropriate expressions of devotion. What could be more touching than that?

And now I have it all—and keep getting more! The gifts you sent . . . were more than enough, like a sweet-smelling sacrifice roasting on the altar, filling the air with fragrance. (Philippians 4:18)

ON GRANDMA'S LAP

▶ Be creative in your gift giving. Some of the best gifts I've given have been inexpensive but something my children or grandchildren have shown an interest in. For example, one Christmas I purchased a pop-up Scotch Tape dispenser for Myles—just like the one on my desk. He was delighted to have his very own source of his favorite sticky stuff. On another occasion Joe bought Web-cams for all three sons so we could see each other (and our grandchildren) when we were chatting online.

▶ Find activities that make your grandchildren laugh, and do them together. See a funny movie, read a silly book, memorize a joke and tell it at the appropriate time. If they are tired, overstimulated by all the holiday hubbub, or feeling a bit homesick, remember that a touch of humor can entirely change the direction of a kid's "Terrible, Horrible, No Good, Very Bad Day."

▶ Tell your grandchildren stories about your family, especially about how they celebrated special holidays. Stories are a great way to help your little ones learn more about their roots and become acquainted with distant relatives they've not known before.

Grandma's Tips

HANDLING HOLIDAY STRESS

▶ Don't let perfection spoil the party. Fussing over details can easily backfire, spoiling the fun for everybody. Your family doesn't care if things are perfect. What they usually appreciate most is traditional fare served in a relaxed atmosphere.

▶ Do as much as you can before the guests arrive. Then delegate some of the chores. Even the grandchildren will enjoy being in on the preparation.

▶ If your family plans to stay several days at your house, suggest a day trip for them—such as visiting a theme park or zoo—and even offer to pay for the excursion. You don't have to go with them to see a landmark you've probably already seen a dozen times. Use the time they're away to prepare the next meal or put your feet up and rest.

▶ Make life easier on yourself by putting away delicate knick-knacks and antiques. It doesn't make sense to display a porcelain nativity scene on the coffee table when there are preschoolers present. Create a kid-friendly environment.

▶ Avoid trying to settle relationship problems during the holidays. They won't go away just because it's Christmas, but they can be addressed later at a less stressful time.

▶ Tune out the hype—all the idealized images of what your house, decorations, and food should be. You probably will not have an *It's a Wonderful Life* experience or a Martha Stewart party, but you will have a great time if you are true to who you are.

▶ Before you reach the point where you don't want to hear one more Christmas song and you're ready to deck someone's turtledove, turn off the radio, go for a short walk, or find some other way to decompress.

TIMELESS TRUTH

The holidays: a time of parties, shopping, religious observances, decorating, family gatherings—and stress. And no wonder! Some of us are just not satisfied with anything less than *the perfect* celebration with all family members present and accounted for. Thankfully, the Word of God gives a solution for this dilemma.

The following verses from the book of Philippians (4:5-9) are taken from the New American Standard Version—my personal favorite. It's amazing how these timeless truths apply to our present-day family situations.

- "Let your gentle spirit be known to all men." Your family will appreciate your attitude when you are accommodating. Do you consider your children's plans as equally important as yours? Are you willing to adapt—to respect their decisions and their boundaries?

- "The Lord is near." He is near in time as well as in proximity. While calendars are helpful to us, they are inconsequential to God. To Him, "one day is like a thousand years, and a thousand years like one day" (2 Peter 3:8, NASB). Our life is "like a passing shadow"[1] in the grand scheme of things. When we understand time from God's point of view, we are able to relax. Knowing He is present brings contentment. Our plans don't seem so all-important when we gain an eternal perspective.

- "Be anxious for nothing . . . " Don't worry about anything—not one thing. Release all your anxious cares, stop fretting over details, let go of all your unrealistic expectations. Your family will be blessed when they see that you are trusting God.
- ". . . but in everything by prayer and supplication with thanksgiving let your requests be made known to God." Bring every detail before God. Tell Him your specific requests, always with an attitude of thanksgiving for His bountiful gifts. "Thanksgiving" is a compound word that is proactive—*giving* Him thanks. Giving always costs something! In fact, thanksgiving involves "sacrifice."[2]

While we may long for our families' attention, our deepest needs are really met in our relationship with God. When we stop expecting our families to be there for us and allow God to take care of our needs, those closest to us will be free to enjoy our company without feeling put upon or stressed out.

- "And the peace of God, which surpasses all comprehension, will guard your hearts and your minds in Christ Jesus." Peace will prevail in your innermost being when you release your anxiety into God's hands. This supernatural peace will guard your heart like a sentinel or warrior, protecting your fragile emotions until you feel safe and find rest deep in your soul.
- "Finally, brethren, whatever is true, whatever is honorable, whatever is right, whatever is pure, whatever is lovely, whatever is of good repute, if there is any excellence and if anything worthy of praise, dwell on these things." When peace prevails, you will be ready to make the following eight steps of progress in

your thinking. God's peace empowers you to radically change the way you think. As you process your thoughts, one step at a time, with each step building upon the previous one, you will find yourself moving upward, experiencing a new sense of freedom. Ask yourself, *Are my thoughts about this situation true? Are my thoughts true and honorable? Are they true, honorable, and right?* And so on.

8. Whatever is worthy of praise . . .

7. Whatever is excellent . . .

6. Whatever is of good repute . . .

5. Whatever is lovely . . .

4. Whatever is pure . . .

3. Whatever is right . . .

2. Whatever is honorable . . .

1. Whatever is true . . .

• "Practice these things, and the God of peace will be with you." *Practice* is a present-tense verb. It means to "make it a continual habit." Anytime you are troubled and tempted to fret, there is something you can do—supplicate by making your requests known to God and then step up to a new way of thinking. When you *practice* these things, you will experience God's peace—no matter what.

Playing Favorites
Without Being Partial

Golden Rule for Siblings: Do one to others
before they do one to you.

—GRACIE MALONE

IT'S A game we've played at our house since my little boys were old enough to talk. One of them would run to me for a hug, and while I was holding them close, I'd whisper, "You're my favorite. You know that, don't you?"

As they became old enough to respond, they sometimes came back in kind: "No, you're *my* favorite."

When Matt and Mike grew into that competitive phase most preschoolers go through, I made a special effort to show equal "favor." (Is that an oxymoron?) They would take turns running to me for a hug, and then I'd overhear them bragging, "I'm her favorite!" "Uh-uh, *I'm* her favorite!" It was a game of playful bantering about who loves whom the most.

When our third son, Jason, came along, it had been twelve years since a baby had occupied a place in our family. I'll admit, at first it was hard not to feel just a tad of actual favoritism toward the "child of my old age" (Genesis 37:3). It's not that I loved his brothers less, but that this little newcomer was so darn cute. Besides that, it felt good to trade car pools, soccer games, garden club, and my chair in the sanctuary choir for the serenity of a rocking chair with a tiny baby on my shoulder, feeling his warm breath as he nuzzled my neck. Jason was, to say the least, *very special*. Thankfully, his older brothers thought so too. He was the Malone Favorite of the Year.

But as soon as he was old enough to walk and talk, the game of Playing Favorites took on a slightly different flavor as we included a third party. "You're my favorite," I'd say as the little tyke toddled toward me. He would grin and reach for a hug. Sometimes, if Matt overheard, he'd come back, "I thought *I* was your favorite." At other times, Mike would get in the act: "I'm the favorite! We all know that." Occasionally, I sensed there might be just a touch of real competitiveness (dare I say jealousy?) between the siblings.

Meanwhile, our boys were busy growing up, literally, in two different worlds. Matt and Mike were caught up in school activities and athletics, while Jason was growing into a precocious kid. We enrolled him in kindergarten the fall after Mike graduated from high school. It wasn't until the older two were away at college that a full-blown case of sibling rivalry broke out. Matt and Mike began to notice their little brother getting more privileges and acquiring more "things" than they had ever had. Eventually, Joe and I found ourselves in hot water when we bought Jason a car.

Now, the kid had already done his time with a clunker. The

family rule was "the first car is a hand-me-down or a not-so-gently-used model." We figured that was a good way to teach a guy how to take care of a motor vehicle without sending his parents into a financial tailspin. Jason's '75 Volkswagen Beetle had lived a long, hard life and died a natural death, and we decided he needed new wheels. The problem was that we bought him *new* wheels. *New*, as in right-off-the-showroom-floor new—a 1993 black Jeep Wrangler. That boy was one cool dude! But as soon as he showed his Jeep to his brothers, I heard grumblings on the home front: "I never got a *new* car!" "A *new* car! Well, isn't that just special!" "Did you also get a coat of many colors?"

Joe and I tried to explain: "Not every parent gets a do-over when it comes to parenting. Jason has given us that opportunity. We want to handle a few things differently than we did the first time around. For one thing, having you guys pay for your own car was a mistake. The part-time jobs you held put too much pressure on you, kept you out late at night, and hurt your grades. Besides that, we're better off financially now and we can afford to provide a car for Jason. Okay, maybe it was a bit much to give him a *new* car, but we're tired of tow trucks and late-night runs to pick up a stranded kid." To be honest, having a car under warranty felt great to a couple of aging parents.

Over a period of time, our explanations (along with a few apologies) seemed to settle the issue. Years later at a family get-together, Matt said, "I remember giving Jason a hard time when he was in high school, but you know what? *Really,* I've always thought I was your favorite—you know, since I was the *firstborn son.*" At that, Mike piped up with "All kidding aside, I honestly thought *I* was—even though I drew *second* place in the family lineup." Jason just grinned and shook his head. After that, I remember thinking how nice it was that all three of our incredible sons felt equally loved—equally "favored." To be sure, we'd made our share of parenting mistakes along the way, but we had also done a few things right. I felt so good realizing my sons had grown into emotionally healthy men that I decided it was safe to continue Playing Favorites. And the game goes on to this day.

Recently, I zipped off an e-mail message to Jason, concluding it with, "You know you're my favorite, don't you?"

It was nothing short of amazing how quickly my words ricocheted through cyberspace. Before long, my computer sounded its "You've Got Mail" tone. There were two messages: One from Matt: "I thought you'd be interested in this message Jason just sent me." And another from Mike: "Hey, Mom, what's this?" I was giggling mischievously as I hit the reply button and sent a reassuring note to both of them: "What was I thinking? *You* are the favorite child." My two messages were identical of course, and I knew without a doubt they'd soon end up on the other guy's computer screen.

While the playful bantering goes on at our house, I realize that in other family circles there are serious issues involving favoritism. And there is nothing funny about it.

My friend Jill has two children, Elizabeth and Joel. Unfortunately, Jill's mother has a favorite—a real, unabashed preference for the granddaughter. One year, this grandmother spent over three hundred dollars for back-to-school clothes for Elizabeth but bought nothing for her preschool grandson. When Joel asked for a new pair of Nike tennis shoes, his grandma chided, "Don't you know how expensive those shoes are?" Jill overheard the conversation but couldn't believe her ears. Elizabeth was sporting a pair of Nikes her grandmother had bought her just a few weeks before. Joel ducked his head and bit his bottom lip. The scenario also made Elizabeth cringe. Later she said, "Mom, I wish Joel had new shoes, too."

Jill simply can't understand her mother. She often wonders, *Is she just clueless? Maybe she can't relate to boys.* Nevertheless, her actions hurt deeply, putting added strain on an already fragile relationship. Jill has tried talking to her mother about these issues, but her concerns seem to fall on deaf ears.

The problem goes deeper than gift giving. This grandmother obviously prefers Elizabeth's gentle, quiet nature to the antics and awkwardness of Joel. Here's how Jill explains what it feels like to take her children to see their grandmother:

Everybody's walking on eggshells, trying not to mess up anything or make too much noise. When we pack up our things and go home, if nothing is broken or soiled, and if the children have behaved well, that's considered a good visit. My mom will actually phone me later and say, "It was such a nice visit; I can't tell anybody's been here."

It hurts to see her priorities so mixed up. I wish grandma's house could be a place where we could let our guard down a bit, relax, and have fun. And it breaks my heart that she doesn't appreciate the fun-loving nature of our little boy. He's not a bad kid; he's just a boy with a high energy level.

Without knowing it, this grandmother's actions have fractured her family. Jill and her husband have had to establish some boundaries to protect Joel from being hurt and to keep their daughter from feeling guilty. The grandparents are no longer invited to birthday celebrations. The family does not spend Christmas together. Joel isn't allowed to spend the night or go on an outing with his grandmother unless one of his parents is present. Jill's mother may not even realize what she has lost, but in my opinion, she's paying a high price for a spotless house.

Jill's situation may seem extreme to you. You may be thinking, "I could never be so cruel, so thoughtless." But there are many grandmothers who struggle with feelings of partiality toward one of their grandchildren. It's hard not to, for invariably one child will have an engaging personality while another rubs the wrong way. Some children are more compliant and loveable, while others are more opinionated or overly active. Sometimes grandmothers feel partial toward a grandchild with special needs. It takes real effort on the part of a sincere grandmother to make sure each child knows he is loved and appreciated for his unique abilities and characteristics, in spite of any faults or weaknesses.

My friend Wanda tries hard to be balanced in the gifts and attention she gives her two granddaughters, who are now young women. She admits feeling partial to the youngest. "When the girls were growing up, it was obvious to me that Megan had not bonded with her mother the way her older sister Caryn had," Wanda explained. "Caryn was truly a mother's girl, loved to be outdoors, enjoyed playing tennis—just like her mom. Megan, on the other hand, loved to read and cook. When they came to see us, she would hang out in the kitchen with me, asking questions and talking nonstop. Feeling partial to this girl I have such an affinity for is something I work on constantly. I don't want to show favoritism, but I feel it every time I'm around my two grandchildren."

If you feel a special closeness to one of your grandchildren, consider what author Erma Bombeck has to say on the matter. She had no problem admitting that she loved each of her three children "best" because of his or her unique characteristics and his or her special place in the family lineup. She wrote a warm tribute to them in one of her newspaper columns.

She claimed to love her firstborn "best" because she was "the genesis of a marriage, the fulfillment of young love." She confessed to loving her second child "best" because he "drew the dumb spot in the family and was stronger for it." He was "the continuance." She loved her youngest "best" because he was "the culmination"—the one of whom she wrote, "You darken our hair, quicken our steps, square our shoulders, restore our vision and give us humor. . . ."[1]

Grandmothers, if you must have favorites, have them for Erma Bombeck-like reasons. It's okay to love your first grandson "best" because he is the beginning of a new generation. Go ahead and love your second granddaughter "best" because her smile reminds you of your mother. Love the third grandson "best" because his mannerisms are so like his daddy's.

But love all your grandchildren equally well because there is something worth loving in every child, something for which you can honestly say, "I favor you because . . . "

> Love one another the way I loved you. This is the
> very best way to love. (John 15:12)

ON GRANDMA'S LAP

▶ Be careful when complimenting the appearance of one grandchild in the presence of another unless you can readily compliment the other child's appearance as well.

▶ If you compliment a trait or gift in one grandchild, try to
  compliment the other(s) within earshot. You might say,
  "Katie, you colored that bunny so beautifully—you are a
  good artist!" and then add, "And Billy is an excellent builder
  with blocks, isn't he? Isn't it wonderful how God gives us each
  a special talent to share with each other?"

▶ Invest in an oversized rocker recliner or a double glider rocker
  so that you can rock one, two, or even three little ones at
  once. Otherwise, make sure you give each child a shot at
  "snuggle time" or "lap time" at some point during the visit,
  and make it clear each child will have his special time.

▶ Make a special date each month or every other month to
  spend time with a grandchild alone. Do things or go to places
  that interest the child so that you can become better
  acquainted with her likes, dislikes, and personality.

▶ Ask God and your spouse to help you project an impartial
  persona around the grandkids. Often a spouse can pick up on
  behaviors or words that could be construed in ways you did
  not intend and can therefore help you avoid unwittingly
  appearing partial.

Grandma's Tips

1. Purchase a soft bathroom rug that has rubber backing. Use this on the living room sofa to create a special place for your grandchild to sit. Not only will the rug protect your furniture, but it will also make your grandchild feel cozy and comfortable. (This also works well for children who are in the process of potty training. You don't have to worry about accidents, and the child will feel less stress too.)

2. Buy your own set of spill-proof cups with tight-fitting lids. Some are designed to accommodate a straw. Several different manufacturers make these cups. Other beverage containers come in cute shapes and sizes. You can also slip a soda straw into a partially opened drink can. Stock up on prepackaged, noncarbonated drinks. They're easy to serve and most of them are *almost* spill-proof. (Avoid drinks that come packaged in foil containers. It's almost impossible for little hands to hold them without the contents squirting all over the kitchen.)

3. One way you can avoid showing partiality is by being consistent in your gift giving. When one child is considerably younger, you can get away with giving an equal *number* of gifts, but when your grandchildren are old enough to understand monetary differences, keep the gifts equal in value. Don't start something for the first grandchild—school shoes every year, a gym set on the first birthday, or a college fund—if you won't be able to do it for all of your grandchildren.

TIMELESS TRUTH

The beautiful love story of Isaac and Rebekah became a tale of espionage, deceit, and revenge after their twin sons, Esau and Jacob, were born. Early in these children's development, differences in their dispositions as well as their likes and dislikes became obvious to their parents. Unfortunately, both parents ended up favoring one child over the other. The scriptural record states:

> The boys grew up. Esau became an expert hunter,
> an outdoorsman. Jacob was a quiet man preferring
> life indoors among the tents. Isaac loved Esau
> because he loved his game, but Rebekah loved
> Jacob. (Genesis 25:27-28)

Esau gave away his rights as firstborn to his younger brother, Jacob, in exchange for a bowl of his tasty stew. Later Jacob tricked his father into giving him Esau's blessing. Jacob's deception led to his banishment from home and separation from his mother. The strife between these two brothers continued throughout their lives. And the pattern of parental favoritism passed into succeeding generations. Jacob became the father of twelve sons, but he had a favorite—Joseph.

> Israel loved Joseph more than any of his other sons
> because he was the child of his old age. And he
> made him an elaborately embroidered coat. When
> his brothers realized that their father loved him
> more than them, they grew to hate him—they
> wouldn't even speak to him. (Genesis 37:3-4)

Joseph endured his brothers' contempt as a result of his father's favoritism. And Jacob grieved for years after the brothers sold Joseph to slave traders and told their father that he was dead.

> Jacob tore his clothes in grief, dressed in rough burlap, and mourned his son a long, long time. His sons and daughters tried to comfort him but he refused their comfort. "I'll go to the grave mourning my son." Oh, how his father wept for him. (Genesis 37:34-35)

Jacob's grief eventually turned into joy when he learned that Joseph was living in Egypt, occupying a place of power second only to the Pharaoh. While our hearts go out to this parent because of his emotional turmoil, we also realize his pain was rooted in his own wrong choices. We are responsible for our own choices, too. The Bible instructs us to honor every person, holding them in high regard, just as our heavenly Father does.

> God plays no favorites! It makes no difference who you are or where you're from—if you want God and are ready to do as he says, the door is open. The Message he sent to the children of Israel—that through Jesus Christ everything is being put together again—well, he's doing it everywhere, among everyone. (Acts 10:34-36)

> It's exactly the same no matter what a person's religious background may be: the same God for all of us, acting the same incredibly generous way to

everyone who calls out for help. "Everyone who
calls, 'Help, God!' gets help." (Romans 10:12-13)

We are also warned about the dangers of comparing one person
to another.

That's why Jesus lived and died and then lived
again: so that he could . . . free us from the petty
tyrannies of each other. (Romans 14:9)

Isn't everything you *have* and everything you *are* sheer
gifts from God? So what's the point of all this comparing and competing? (1 Corinthians 4:7)

In all this comparing and grading and competing,
they quite miss the point. (2 Corinthians 10:12)

We will not compare ourselves with each other as if
one of us were better and another worse. We have
far more interesting things to do with our lives. Each
of us is an original. (Galatians 5:26)

Think of each of your grandchildren, with their good qualities
as well as their quirks and idiosyncrasies, as an original masterpiece in progress, a work of art on God's easel.

From One Generation to the Next

Be nice to your children, for they will pick your nursing home.
—PHYLLIS DILLER

WHEN OUR son Mike planned to be out of town for a week, Jeanna invited me to spend a few days with her and our grandsons, Montana and Myles. We had a great time sleeping late, shopping, eating out, and playing with the kids. But the thing I enjoyed most was having regular late-night chats with my daughter-in-law. Once the children were tucked snuggly in their beds, Jeanna and I would put on our pajamas, stoke the fire in the fireplace, pop some corn, and talk till the wee hours of the morning like two high school girlfriends.

Jeanna and I are able to talk about almost anything, including religion, politics, and family—especially family. We communicate quite well now, but it hasn't always been so. In fact, the first time I met Jeanna, she was so shy she had trouble saying a complete sentence in my presence. When Mike introduced her, she extended her hand and managed a polite "glad to meet you," then quickly sat down on the stairs just inside our front door, folding her arms tightly around her knees. I remember thinking, *She looks like a scared puppy — a cute puppy, but a frightened one nevertheless.* I also recall wondering what I could do to make her feel more comfortable.

After a few moments, I plopped down on the stairs beside her and, in the gentlest voice I could conjure, asked a few get-acquainted questions. Believe me, it takes real effort for me to come on slowly, listen well, and resist the urge to finish another person's sentences. But I knew my usual gregarious manner would send this subdued girl running to her own backyard in a hurry. And the look on Mike's face had already convinced me that Jeanna was "a keeper."

Nevertheless, I had a few legitimate concerns. In my next conversation with Mike, I was not quite as tactful. "Are you sure you want to *marry* this girl?" I began. "She's just so reserved and all. Do you really think she'll fit in with our boisterous family?" Mike grinned and answered, "But, Mom, isn't she pretty?" His reply had absolutely nothing to do with my question, so I came back in a perturbed tone, "Yes, she's pretty! But, Mike, someday you might want to *talk* to her!" As best I can remember, that comment abruptly ended our conversation, but fortunately, it didn't end the relationship between Jeanna and Mike. Before long, he brought her to see us again.

This time Jeanna made it to the couch before collapsing in a crumpled heap. I sat beside her and, once again, exercised all the self-control I could muster as we took our first baby steps toward a meaningful relationship. Eventually, Jeanna and Mike married and produced two amazing sons — Montana and Myles. And, believe me, not one member of that family has trouble talking. In fact, the other day it was Jeanna who was complaining about the lack of meaningful conversation. "Mike," she whined, "why don't you ever talk to me? You know, tell me how you *feel?*" I've only got one thing to say about that: *Who'd a thunk it?*

Ten years after those first social encounters, I made the aforementioned trip to visit this little family in The Woodlands near Houston. The conversations between my daughter-in-law and me were warm, thought provoking, and downright fun.

One night, for example, Jeanna confided, "Gracie, I felt so bad about something that happened this morning while I was getting ready to go to the store. I heard a loud crash coming from the bathroom, followed by a blood-curdling scream. Then Montana began crying so loudly, I just knew he had broken an arm or cut himself badly. I ran as fast as I could from the kitchen into the bathroom. I didn't know what I'd see when I rounded that corner."

"Oh my goodness!" I interjected. "What happened?"

"Well," Jeanna took a deep breath. "When I got there, Montana was draped across the side of the bathtub, the shower curtain was crumpled around him, and he was clutching a piece of broken plastic. You know that gadget that holds our shampoo and soap? Seems he had been swinging on it like it was a jungle gym. When it broke, he fell and landed on his back, right on the side of the tub. Anyway, other than a bad bruise, he seems to be okay. But we were both so scared!"

"Well, honey," I said, "accidents like that happen—especially with little boys like ours. Why do you feel bad about it? You know, mothers can't be everywhere."

"Oh, I know that," Jeanna murmured. "It's just that, well, I didn't respond the way I wish I had." She paused. "Oh, Gracie, I'm so ashamed. When I burst through that door and realized he was okay, I said a four-letter word. I really let one fly! In fact, I yelled so loud it stopped the crying and made Montana's eyes bug out."

"It's okay." I patted her on the leg sympathetically. "What happened after that?"

"Well, I apologized, of course. But I know he won't forget what I said. I just wish I could take it back."

"Your reaction was pretty normal. And you've handled it the best you could," I said. "Montana's forgiven you; now you need to forgive yourself." I wanted to tell her that Montana wouldn't remember the word, but, alas, I'd already heard the story from the perspective of a four-year-old kid.

"Grandma Gracie, my mom said a bad word," Montana had whispered.

"Well, I'm sure she's sorry about that. You know, son, sometimes grown-ups make mistakes, just like kids do. I know she feels badly about it. You need to forgive your mother."

"Yeah." He shrugged and then added something that made *my* eyes bug out. "Grandma Gracie, she said the "F" word." I felt my blood pressure rising as I thought, *This kid's too young to know such a word even exists.* But I had yet to hear the whole story.

"Grandma Gracie, do you know what the "F" word is?" Montana asked.

"I think I do." I swallowed hard and asked, "Do you?"

"Yep!" he picked at a string on his jeans for several minutes. "I'll tell you what the 'F' word is if you promise not to go *Aghhhhhhhhh!*" (I couldn't help but grin as I thought, *That kid knows his grandma so well!*)

Now, I ask you, what would you have done? I promised! "Tell me, Montana. What is the 'F' word?" I braced myself.

Montana wiped his forehead, exhaled loudly, and shook his head a couple of times. I could tell this kid really hated to tell on his mom. But, after a long pause, he cupped his hand around his mouth and, in a subdued tone, spat out the word: *"Butt!"*

I jumped and ran out of the room. I needed a place where I could giggle without little eyes observing and gather my wits about me. I should have remembered Montana was too young to spell. Why, he barely knew the alphabet! But somewhere he'd heard the phrase "'F' word," and I guess he figured all bad words fit into some sort of "F" category. I decided it was time to tell his mother what he had said. Besides, it was too good a story to keep to myself.

As we sat huddled on the sofa in front of the fire, Jeanna and I laughed shamelessly. Then we launched into a long discussion about reactions and how to handle them. I reminded her of something I'd recently read in the Bible, "We get it wrong nearly every time we open our mouths. If you could find someone whose speech was perfectly true, you'd have a perfect person, in perfect control of life" (James 3:2).

"It's not easy to control what we say," I explained, "especially when it comes to a knee-jerk reaction. I've mumbled a few bad words myself at times. Because neither of us is anywhere near perfect, I guess we'll be working on this problem for a long time."

Five days later, I loaded my car for the trip back home. As Jeanna and I stood in the driveway saying a long good-bye, I thought about how far we'd come. When we hugged each other, the embrace lasted longer than usual. Then I felt a sob coming from deep within her tiny frame. "What's wrong, Jeanna?" I asked. Black mascara was pooling beneath her big, brown eyes. "I don't want you to go," she blubbered. "I'm going to miss you."

Tears filled my eyes as we hugged again, patting each other on the shoulders. Then I felt my wacky sense of humor bubbling to the surface. "Jeanna," I giggled as I wiped a tear, "it's not like I live in West Africa or something. Remember you're coming to Dallas in three weeks." At that, we both laughed, hard.

"I love you, Gracie," Jeanna said.

"I love you, too!"

Jeanna wiped her eyes with the bottom of her T-shirt and added, "Before you go, I want to say something."

I waited, swallowing a lump in my throat while she gained her composure.

"You're my example of the person I want to be," she began. "I'm looking at you, learning from you—how to be a good mother, how to be a good wife. I want my little boys to grow up to be like your boys. You know," she shuffled from one foot to the other and pushed her hands into the pockets of her jeans, "I want them to have strong values, to be good men, great daddies—*just like Mike.*"

I smiled as I thought, *What a great friend that gal has become!* My second thought was, *If that doesn't put pressure on a person, I don't know what does!* "Thank you, Jeanna," I stammered. "I'm trying to be a good model, but I've made my share of mistakes along the way. . . . "

At this point, Jeanna interrupted. "Well, if you didn't goof up once in a while, I wouldn't love you."

During the four hours it took me to drive home, I thought about how Jeanna and I had managed to get from where we once were to the place we now share. Then my thoughts turned to my own mother. (At ninety-three years young, she is still my mentor and friend. Even though at times she forgets the names of my children, she still comes up with tidbits of homespun wisdom that amaze and inspire me.) I thought about how she helped me when my kids were growing up—sometimes with practical help and at other times by simply providing encouragement.

I remember one time in particular. Our sons had reached the troublesome teen years, a time when most mothers wonder if they've done anything right. I had confided to my mom some of my concerns. Then I asked, "Mother, you raised six kids who've turned out to be decent, loving people. I know you worried about all of us at times, but when I was growing up, I don't remember you ever being downcast or negative. How did you manage to keep your sweet, positive attitude?"

"Well, Gracie," she began, "I just focus on the good things— count my blessings. You know, like the old hymn reminds us to do." She smiled as she recited the words: "Count your blessings, name them one by one. Count your blessings, see what God has done." Then she added, "You know, my six children are the greatest blessings I have."

I felt my emotions soar to a new level as I thought about the blessings my boys have brought to my life. Then I pictured my mother as she was in years past, surrounded by a roomful of clamoring children, yet having all the serenity of a saint as she focused on her "blessings" instead of her problems. Her simple advice was enough to change my focus as well.

As I drove home, I remembered something my sister, Lois, had told me. When her daughter-in-law Frances signed the adoption papers and picked up Lois's granddaughter at the hospital nursery, the baby was just three days old. A few days later, as Lois and Frances stood beside little Jennifer's crib, the weight of raising the child seemed overwhelming to the inexperienced mother. Lois put her arm around Frances' shoulders and said, "Don't worry, Frances. If we put everything *I know* and everything *you know* together, we should be able to raise one heck of a smart girl!" And you know what? Today that little girl is a charming, beautiful, *and smart* young woman.

Parenting works beautifully when tidbits of sage wisdom, liberal doses of old-fashioned common sense, and armloads of love are handed down from one generation to the next. It doesn't "take a village" to raise a child. It takes a family.

> Even when I am old and gray, do not forsake me, O God, till I declare your power to the next generation, your might to all who are to come. (Psalm 71:18, NIV)

ON GRANDMA'S LAP

▶ Talk to your grandchildren about members of the preceding generations. They will love to hear stories about the games your mother played or the adventures you shared with your daddy. (My children love the story I tell about my mother's brothers— their great uncles, Herman and Cecil. One day, these two boys climbed on top of the barn, carrying an old umbrella. Herman opened the umbrella and jumped off, hoping it would work like a parachute. It didn't. He landed in a stack of hay and, amazingly enough, was able to limp back to the house.)

► Don't be afraid to tell your children and grandchildren the truth about yourself, including some of your own struggles, mistakes, and blunders. You don't have to present a perfect, "I've got it all together" image. Nobody can relate to perfectionism. If you want members of your family to open up about their problems and seek your advice or help, you must share a few of your imperfections as well.

► Discuss the faith of your forefathers so your grandchildren will know about the beliefs and convictions of former generations. This will help them come to their own conclusions about important spiritual matters. The apostle Paul reminisced about his relationship with his young protégé, Timothy, and revealed the impact family had upon his spiritual development: "That precious memory triggers another: your honest faith—and what a rich faith it is, handed down from your grandmother Lois to your mother Eunice, and now to you!" (2 Timothy 1:5).

Grandma's Tips

HOW CHILDREN LEARN

1. They learn from stories. Tell your grandchildren lots of stories—family stories, stories about God, Bible stories. I still remember the Bible stories I learned as a child: Noah's ark filled to the roof with all sorts of animal pairs; the building of the Tower of Babel when people tried to touch the clouds with their construction; the story of David, a little shepherd boy, facing off

to do battle with a giant, using only a sling and five smooth stones. Jesus set the example of teaching truth by using stories. In fact he seldom spoke without telling a story.[1]

2. They learn by example. Grandparents should model character traits they want their grandchildren to develop. The apostle Paul instructed the believers in Corinth with words that grandparents today can pass on to their grandchildren: "Follow my example, as I follow the example of Christ" (1 Corinthians 11:1, NIV).

▶ Model God's love—a love not based on achievement, but an unconditional love that *just is*.

▶ Model God's grace and mercy—Dr. Paul Warren defines grace as "receiving more blessings than you deserve" and mercy as "receiving less punishment than you deserve."[2]

▶ Model honesty and truth. If your grandchildren see you fudging on the truth or being dishonest in some of your dealings, it will affect their concept of truth as well as their behavior.

▶ Model the reality of your faith and trust. Do you depend on God? Are your grandchildren aware of how much you trust His guidance and inner support?

▶ Model your faith with your words and with the way you spend your time. Your grandchildren will know what occupies a place of high priority in your life.

TIMELESS TRUTH

There's a list of ways in the New Testament book of Titus that describes how older women can influence and encourage younger women. Even though these concepts were written a long time ago to address problems in the church at Crete, they are issues that women in our society encounter on a daily basis.

It's interesting to note that while the pastor was supposed to handle most problems this group of believers faced, the training of the young women was delegated to the mature women in the congregation. It's a good plan, both then and now.

After all, who knows the unique needs, problems, and emotions women face better than another woman? Besides that, women are capable of deep, intimate friendships with each other—relationships that provide the perfect soil for healthy spiritual growth. The more mature women, those who have experienced God's grace in its various forms and who've accumulated wisdom through all sorts of experiences in life, are given the privilege and responsibility of helping upcoming generations. Even today, young women need role models and mentors.

Six specific areas of concern are mentioned in the following verses:

> Guide older women into lives of reverence so they end up
> . . . models of goodness. By looking at them, the younger
> women will know how to love their husbands and chil-
> dren, be virtuous and pure, keep a good house, be good
> wives. We don't want anyone looking down on God's
> Message because of their behavior. (Titus 2:3-5)

- Mentors are able to show young women "how to love their husbands" so that they become close, intimate friends—companions in the truest sense of the word.

> > Friends love through all kinds of weather,
> > and families stick together in all kinds of
> > trouble. (Proverbs 17:17)

> Two are better than one,
>> because they have a good return for their work:
> If one falls down,
>> his friend can help him up.
> But pity the man who falls
>> and has no one to help him up!
> Also, if two lie down together, they will keep warm.
>> But how can one keep warm alone?
> Though one may be overpowered,
>> two can defend themselves.
> A cord of three strands is not quickly broken.
> (Ecclesiastes 4:9-12, NIV)

- Young women need guidance and practical help in order to "love their children" well.

> I'll let you in on the sweet old truths,
> Stories we heard from our fathers,
>> counsel we learned at our mother's knee.
> We're not keeping this to ourselves,
>> we're passing it along to the next generation—
> GOD's fame and fortune,
>> the marvelous things he has done.
> He planted a witness in Jacob,
>> set his Word firmly in Israel,
> Then commanded our parents
>> to teach it to their children
> So the next generation would know,
>> and all the generations to come—
> Know the truth and tell the stories
>> so their children can trust in God. (Psalm 78:2-7)

- Older women have a different and much-needed perspective on what it means "to live a virtuous life." *Virtuous* means self-controlled, having an inner self-government that enables one to think like Christ, to see life as Christ would see it.

> Take your everyday, ordinary life—your sleeping,
> eating, going-to-work, and walking-around life—and
> place it before God as an offering. Embracing what
> God does for you is the best thing you can do for
> him. Don't become so well-adjusted to your culture
> that you fit into it without even thinking. Instead, fix
> your attention on God. You'll be changed from the
> inside out. Readily recognize what he wants from
> you, and quickly respond to it. Unlike the culture
> around you, always dragging you down to its level of
> immaturity, God brings the best out of you, develops
> well-formed maturity in you. (Romans 12:1-3)

- Young women need someone to teach them "how to be
  pure"—to be an example of good character.

> As obedient children, let yourselves be pulled into a
> way of life shaped by God's life, a life energetic and
> blazing with holiness. God said, "I am holy; you be
> holy." (1 Peter 1:15-16)

> Be good wives to your husbands, responsive to their
> needs. There are husbands who, indifferent as they
> are to any words about God, will be captivated by
> your life of holy beauty. What matters is not your
> outer appearance—the styling of your hair, the jew-
> elry you wear, the cut of your clothes—but your
> inner disposition. Cultivate inner beauty, the gentle,

gracious kind that God delights in. (1 Peter 3:1-4)

- Older women are able to teach younger women "to keep a good house." Wives are the "home management specialists" of our day, experts at making things work well at home. Home should be a sanctuary where every member of the family feels safe and comfortable, a place where each person can count on being heard, finding help, and getting a hug.

> It takes wisdom to build a house,
>   and understanding to set it on a firm foundation;
> It takes knowledge to furnish its rooms
>   with fine furniture and beautiful draperies.
>   (Proverbs 24:3-4)

> If God doesn't build the house,
>   the builders only build shacks. (Psalm 127:1)

- Younger wives are looking for older, living examples to teach them how to "be good wives." These verses are about structure in the family and describe the different roles and responsibilities of husbands and wives.

> Haven't you read in your Bible that the Creator origi-
> nally made man and woman for each other, male
> and female? And because of this, a man leaves father
> and mother and is firmly bonded to his wife, becom-
> ing one flesh—no longer two bodies but one.
> Because God created this organic union of the two
> sexes, no one should desecrate his art by cutting

them apart. . . . Not everyone is mature enough to
live a married life. It requires a certain aptitude and
grace. Marriage isn't for everyone. . . . But if you're
capable of growing into the largeness of marriage, do
it. (Matthew 19:4-6,11-12)

Wives, understand and support your husbands in
ways that show your support for Christ. The husband provides leadership to his wife the way Christ
does to his church, not by domineering but by cher-
ishing. So just as the church submits to Christ as he
exercises such leadership, wives should likewise
submit to their husbands. Husbands, go all out in
your love for your wives, exactly as Christ did for
the church—a love marked by giving, not getting.
Christ's love makes the church whole. His words
evoke her beauty. Everything he does and says is
designed to bring the best out of her, dressing her
in dazzling white silk, radiant with holiness. And
that is how husbands ought to love their wives.
They're really doing themselves a favor—since
they're already "one" in marriage. No one abuses his
own body, does he? No, he feeds and pampers it.
That's how Christ treats us, the church, since we are
part of his body. And this is why a man leaves father
and mother and cherishes his wife. No longer two,
they become "one flesh." This is a huge mystery,
and I don't pretend to understand it all. What is

clearest to me is the way Christ treats the church.
And this provides a good picture of how each husband is to treat his wife, loving himself in loving
her, and how each wife is to honor her husband.
(Ephesians 5:22-33)

The apostle Paul, author of the book of Titus, knew the incredible power of a woman. He understood that when women model
these concepts well, God's Message is honored.

Appendix

The ABCs of God's Word

WHEN OUR youngest son became a toddler, I put together a small book to help him memorize verses from the Bible. I traced around each of his colorful, magnetic Fisher Price alphabet letters on a 3 x 5 card, typed a verse that fit with the letter, punched holes in the cards, and put them in a small three-ring binder. I colored the alphabet in his book the same color as the plastic piece, making them color-coded to the toy letters. The little book became one of our son's favorites. He would play with the plastic letters, fitting them on top of my hand-drawn ones, comparing the colors. And as he played, I would help him say the verses. Sometimes he would place the letters on the refrigerator door as we quoted the verses he had learned. The little book became a valuable tool for teaching the timeless truths of Scripture to our little boy.

These verses were carefully selected to teach important concepts, not simply because they begin with a certain letter of the alphabet. I have updated my selections using the NIV translation of the Bible, except where identified differently.

A "For ALL have sinned and fall short of the glory of God" (Romans 3:23).

B "Everything is possible for him who BELIEVES" (Mark 9:23).

C "CAST all your anxiety on him because he cares for you" (1 Peter 5:7).

D "DELIGHT yourself in the LORD and he will give you the desires of your heart" (Psalm 37:4).

E "In EVERY THING give thanks" (1 Thessalonians 5:18, KJV).

F "FEAR the LORD and shun evil" (Proverbs 3:7).

G "My GRACE is sufficient for you, for my power is made perfect in weakness" (2 Corinthians 12:9).

H "Be HOLY, because I am holy" (1 Peter 1:16).

I "God said to Moses, 'I AM WHO I AM'" (Exodus 3:14).

J "The JUST shall live by his faith (Habakkuk 2:4, KJV).

K "Be KIND and compassionate to one another" (Ephesians 4:32).

L "LOVE one another. As I have loved you, so you must love one another" (John 13:34).

M "Blessed are the merciful, for they will be shown MERCY" (Matthew 5:7).

N "I will do whatever you ask in my NAME" (John 14:13).

O "Children, OBEY your parents in the Lord, for this is right" (Ephesians 6:1).

P "The testing of your faith develops PERSEVERANCE" (James 1:3).

Q "In QUIETNESS and trust is your strength" (Isaiah 30:15).

R "RESIST the devil, and he will flee from you" (James 4:7).

S "SIN shall not have dominion over you" (Romans 6:14, KJV).

T "TRUST in the LORD with all your heart" (Proverbs 3:5).

U "UNDERSTAND what the Lord's will is" (Ephesians 5:17).

V "Add to your faith VIRTUE" (2 Peter 1:5, KJV).

W "They that WAIT upon the LORD shall renew their strength" (Isaiah 40:31, KJV).

X "Be thou an EXAMPLE of the believers, in word, in conversation, in charity, in spirit, in faith, in purity" (1 Timothy 4:12, KJV).

Y "YIELD yourselves unto God" (Romans 6:13, KJV).

Z Be "ZEALOUS of good works" (Titus 2:14, KJV).

Notes

GRANDMOTHERS THEN AND NOW

1. Poem taken from *Courage for the Chicken Hearted*, 1998 by Becky Freeman, Susan Duke, Rebecca Barlow Jordan, Gracie Malone, and Fran Caffey Sandin. Used by permission of Honor Books.

CHAPTER 2

1. See Revelation 2:17.

CHAPTER 3

1. Dr. Paul Warren, *My Preschooler: Ready for New Adventures* (Nashville: Thomas Nelson, 1994), p. 92.
2. John Trent, Ph.D., Rick Osborne, and Kurt Bruner, *Parents' Guide to the Spiritual Growth of Children: Helping Your Child Develop a Personal Faith* (Wheaton, Ill.: Tyndale, 2000), p. 116.
3. Becky Freeman, *Still Lickin' the Spoon (And Other Confessions of a Grown-Up Kid)* (Nashville: Broadman & Holman, 1997), p. 6.

CHAPTER 5

1. Excerpts taken from *Courage for the Chicken Hearted*, 1998 by Becky Freeman, Susan Duke, Rebecca Barlow Jordan, Gracie Malone, and Fran Caffey Sandin. Used by permission of Honor Books.

CHAPTER 6

1. Julie Ann Barnhill, *She's Gonna Blow!: Real Help for Moms Dealing with Anger* (Eugene, Ore.: Harvest House, 2001), p. 36.
2. See Psalm 23:4, NIV.

3. See Proverbs 10:13; 23:13-14; 29:15,17, NIV.
4. Compare Isaiah 10:5.

CHAPTER 7

1. See Ephesians 5:16.

CHAPTER 8

1. See John 8:32.

CHAPTER 10

1. See Psalm 144:4, NASB; see also Psalm 39:5, Psalm 102:11.
2. See Hebrews 13:15.

CHAPTER 11

1. Erma Bombeck, *Forever, Erma* (Kansas City, Mo.: Andrews McMeel, 1996), pp. 38-39.

CHAPTER 12

1. See Matthew 13:34-35.
2. Dr. Paul Warren, *My Preschooler: Ready for New Adventures* (Nashville: Thomas Nelson, 1994), p. 196.

About the Author

IT WASN'T until after her youngest son headed off to college that Gracie mailed an article she'd written to a magazine. She wondered if *just maybe* they'd be interested in publishing it. They were! (There's life after kids.) Her first article came out in *Moody* magazine in 1994. Since then, Gracie's work has been published several times in *Moody* in addition to other well-known magazines, including *Discipleship Journal, Decision, Women Alive, Christian Parenting Today, Home Life,* and *Celebrate Life.* One of her articles won the "Best Article" award at the 1997 Florida Christian Writer's Conference.

Courage for the Chicken Hearted (Honor Books, 1998), Gracie's first book project, coauthored with four friends affectionately dubbed "Hens with Pens," quickly became a best-seller. The success of her first book encouraged its sequel the next year, *Eggstra Courage for the Chicken Hearted.* Recently both books were reprinted by Guideposts in a hardbound, two-volume set. They've also been published in Korean. Gracie has contributed to several other books, including the Women of Faith compilation, *She Who Laughs, Lasts.*

In addition to her writing, Gracie is a Bible study teacher, precept leader, and much-loved speaker for women's conferences and retreats. A pastor reported, "Through her Bible studies, Gracie literally became a mentor to women throughout our entire county. She is real, transparent, loving, biblical, and humorous—a gifted communicator."

Gracie and her husband, Joe, live in Grapevine, Texas, near their children and grandchildren.

"Speak Up with Confidence," a speakers' bureau managed by Gene and Carol Kent, handles her speaking ministry. You may contact them at www.speakupinc@aol.com or by phone at 888-870-7719. You can find Gracie online at www.graciemalone.com, by e-mail at gracie@graciemalone.com, or by phone/fax at 817-488-2317.

BOOKS FOR EVERY STAGE OF A WOMAN'S LIFE.

The Intentional Woman

Feeling a bit lost? Rediscover who God made you to be and begin to track a path toward a meaningful and God-honoring life.

(Carol Travilla and Joan Webb)

What Will I Do with the Rest of My Life?

This dynamic book will help you see life after 40 as a new beginning full of immense possibilities and an exciting new sense of direction. And you'll discover that God's best for you is yet to come!

(Brenda Poinsett)

Becoming a Woman of Influence

If you want your life to count for eternity, this book will help you learn to have a lasting, godly impact on other people's lives.

(Carol Kent)

Choosing Rest

Author Sally Breedlove shows us how to choose God's perfect gift of rest, even in the midst of our restless lives.

(Sally Breedlove)

To get your copies, visit your local bookstore, call 1-800-366-7788, or log on to www.navpress.com. Ask for a FREE catalog of NavPress products. Offer #BPA.

NAVPRESS

BRINGING TRUTH TO LIFE
www.navpress.com